Everything Your Coach Never Told You Because You're a Girl

and other truths about winning

BY DAN BLANK

ISBN: 0989697746
ISBN 13: 9780989697743

This book is dedicated to all the players I've ever coached who genuinely believed there was no such thing as an unwinnable game.

TABLE OF CONTENTS

"Well-behaved women seldom make history."
Laurel Thatcher Ulrich

INTRODUCTION

Okay, you're a girl, you play a sport and you want to win and win a lot. Fabulous!

The problem is that, well… you're a girl. That means coaches don't talk to you the same way they talk to boys. You're the recipient of a nice little double standard in which the world lowers its expectations of you because of your gender. Chances are that every coach you've ever had softened his message to you because you're a girl and not a boy. Let me tell you something: *That stops right now.*

I'm going to let you in on a little secret: When it's time to play, I don't care how nice you are. I don't care that you made the Dean's List or volunteered as a candy striper or saved a whale. When it's game time, all I really care about is that you do everything in your power to win the stinkin' game. Got it?

I'm going to teach you everything I know about winning. And I'm going to weave these lessons into the story of a group of soccer players I coached at a small NAIA school in Daytona Beach. Why? *Because they got it.* They weren't super talented or super athletic, but when it came to competition, they totally got it. They aren't celebrities. You won't know their names and you haven't seen them on television, but don't be misled. Inside the bubble in which we lived, these girls became notorious for their willingness to do whatever was necessary to win.

Eventually I left that school and moved on to become a Division I coach. As I write this book, I have been a Division I coach for seven years. I could hide behind the Division I label and write about the players I've coached at a much more high-profile university, but I'm not going to do that. Why not? Because this book isn't so much about what I taught a group of female soccer players; it's about what they taught me. It's all those lessons I learned from observing a group of players that overachieved on such a grand scale that their achievements deserved to be documented. I want to give credit where credit is due.

Many of the players you're about to meet weren't highly recruited by the nation's top programs because they were flawed in some form or fashion — they weren't big enough or fast enough or talented enough. And most of them didn't fit the girl-next-door image that we prefer in our female athletes. These girls were hardly typical. They were renegades and hellions and misfits. They weren't afraid to color outside of the lines, and no one ever accused them of compassion — at least not during a soccer game. They were loud and obnoxious and funny and they didn't care what you thought about them. They became the most hated team in the Florida Sun Conference because that's exactly what they wanted. But make no mistake about it — they were winners — and you can learn a lot from them.

It's time for you to stop worrying about the way you're supposed to act and to start focusing on the way to bury your opponents. So, let's take off the kid gloves and start talking to you like a competitor instead of talking to you like a girl.

PART 1
GETTING IT

There are many coaches who are excellent at teaching the game. They are superb at helping you to improve technically, tactically and physically. Those coaches make you a better player. But make no mistake about it, there's a difference between being a player and being a competitor. Most athletes strike some type of balance between the two. But winners, regardless of their level of technical/tactical/physical ability, always have their competitive gas pedal pinned to the floor. When game time arrives, those other abilities are stagnant. You won't become magically faster, smarter or more talented between the first whistle and the last. In order to impose yourself on the contest at maximum volume, you've got to maximize your competitive fury. Let me put it to you another way: *All other things being equal, the competitor beats the player.*

The game you play exists in a bubble, and you need to compartmentalize it accordingly. If you want to succeed in the theater of competition, then you have to make peace with the rules of engagement that exist in that theater. You have to rid yourself of that tiny voice that keeps nagging you; the one that says you must always work and play well with others. You've got to give yourself permission to do what is necessary to win. If you don't, believe me, you're going to lose to the competitor who does.

1

Getting It

I 've been coaching female athletes for 24 years and I believe they can be neatly divided into two groups: those who get it, and those who don't. The ones who don't get it far outnumber those who do. That's why coaches are so elated when a player who *gets it* ends up on their roster. Those are the players that win championships.

The ones who don't get it are programmed to complicate their existence as athletes because they've never truly figured out the purpose of competition. They are forever walking an impossible high-wire, struggling to find a balance between competitiveness and relationships and being the girl that society wants them to be. Their competitive life is a never-ending compromise, a search for a comfortable middle-ground so that their desire to conquer won't threaten their social status or their relationships with teammates.

That compromise dilutes their value as competitors. Although their competitive volume has the capacity of reaching ten, they won't turn the dial above seven. Instead of charging mightily into the arena of competition, they are always dragging one foot in a puddle of mediocrity.

The beautiful few who get it are not hamstrung by this compromise. They have no problem separating their off-field relationships from their competitive duties. The two entities exist in two separate containers. They can be great competitors and they can be wonderful friends. They are hardly ever both at the exact same moment.

There is one very simple element that separates those who get it from those who don't: *The ones who get it fully grasp that the very simple premise of competition is to separate the winner from the loser.* That's it.

The ones who get it have this premise digested. It dictates the way they approach competition during matches and training sessions. It categorizes their relationships with teammates — relationships that differ radically between moments of competition and all other moments. They don't bow to anyone during the throes of competition. They play to win because regardless of what you've been told, winning is in fact the end-all, be-all of competition.

The primary purpose of this book is to teach those who want to get it, *how to get it.*

I am a women's college soccer coach. My job is to teach young women that they have every right to want to win as much as men do, that they don't need permission to do what is necessary to achieve victory and that they should never apologize for conquering an opponent.

From 1998-2006, I served as the women's soccer coach at Embry-Riddle Aeronautical University. Due to the specialized academic curriculum of our university and our limited amount of scholarships, one thing was guaranteed: We would never be as talented as the best teams in the nation. We didn't have the academic curriculum to attract the very best players, nor the scholarship money to buy them. To beat those teams and many others, we needed to maximize the tools that we had. And the most powerful tool at our disposal was always going to be our attitude - our *conscious* choices.

Although we were challenged by our academic curriculum and scholarship budget, our program won a lot of games and championships. This is how we did it.

2

Winning the Parking Lot

Darkness was settling in on Ft. Lauderdale as our team bus turned into the parking lot of the Hilton Hotel and crept to a stop. Elizabeth Fisher rose from her seat and announced to her teammates, "Nobody move!"

On the surface, Fish was *the-girl-next-door*. With straight blonde hair, soft blue eyes and a friendly face, Fish was positively approachable. She was kind and gentle with an easy smile – the kind that can only come from a warm heart. Like her teammates, Fish wore a dress that night – proper attire for the Region 14 Championship Tournament banquet. But regardless of how she smiled or how she dressed or how warm her heart was, when it came to soccer, Fish was an assassin.

As her teammates waited in their seats, Fish walked up to the front of the bus and stood beside our driver. One of our competitors' busses had already arrived and parked in one of the four spots reserved for busses. Our driver, Bill, had the option of pulling up beside that bus or tucking in behind it. He chose to tuck in behind it. That's when Fish stood up. Now at the front, she leaned over his shoulder.

"Bill," she said politely, "You've always been our favorite driver and we're happy you're with us this weekend, but don't ever park us behind another team's bus. We plan on winning everything this weekend and that includes the parking at this banquet. Now pull us up beside that other bus, and make sure we park a little bit ahead of it."

Bill, a kind man late into his sixties, did as Fish instructed, parking our bus a nose past our opponent's. From my seat in the front row, I hid my grin and thought *YES!*

Fish arrived as a decent, hard-working soccer player with a good attitude. But it was in our program that she developed that edge that took her from being a decent soccer player to being an unapologetic conqueror. As her career was winding down, it was clear that somewhere along the way, Fish had figured out how to become a winner.

As Bill was maneuvering our bus into its new parking spot, I knew we were about to win our first regional championship.

3

What is a Winner?

In 1997 I was speaking with one of the coaches of the U.S. U-21 women's national soccer team that had just won the Nordic Cup. She was going into detail about the different players on the U.S. roster. One player she spoke of was Tiffany Roberts, a rising star in the national team system. This is how the coach described Roberts:

"She's not the most technical player, but that kid is a winner. She totally refuses to lose. You tell her to win, and she goes out and wins."

Now this coach, who had the luxury of choosing her team from the most talented U-21 players in the country, was telling me that although Roberts wasn't as technically gifted as some players who didn't make the team, her commitment to winning made her indispensable. That commitment is also what made Roberts an Olympic gold medalist. The description of Tiffany Roberts would forever stick with me.

Dan Barlow is the strength and conditioning coach for Real Salt Lake in Major League Soccer. While Tiffany Roberts was skyrocketing to soccer stardom, Dan was serving as a strength and conditioning coach at the University of Maryland. He worked mainly with the Terps' football and basketball players, but one day the women's lacrosse coach asked Dan to speak to her team. Dan summed up the experience succinctly: "They were different."

He didn't mean they were different from men; he meant they were different, very different, from the other female athletes he had worked with. Dan said, "I walked over to the field and they all had this look on their face like, 'You better be able to teach me something or otherwise get out of here because you are wasting my time.' I've never gotten a colder reception from a team of women."

Yes, the Terps were different. Their mentality was different. Their view of competition was different. It was that mentality that guided them to five straight national titles from 1995-1999, a span that included a 50-game winning streak. That type of extended excellence doesn't just materialize because of talented players, and it doesn't happen by accident. It is the byproduct of a culture that treasures competitive supremacy. A culture like that is not easy to create or maintain, and it is certainly not common. That type of winning culture is *different*.

Even when I had been coaching women for more than a decade, I still couldn't pinpoint that intangible quality that separates the winners from the rest of the field. All I knew for sure was that when it came to competitions, the winners found a way to win. It wasn't until recently that I realized precisely what it is that separates the winners from the herd. It hit me like a bolt of lightning and all at once it became very clear. There is a simple formula for winning, and I'm going to reveal it to you in a later chapter. The great news is that it is something each one of us has the power to control. And like so many of the principles you are about to read, it is as simple as making a conscious decision.

4

Winners Win...
and Winners Win

Winners win... and winners win... By 2002, that was a common saying in our program at Embry-Riddle. Rarely a day went by when someone didn't mention it. But it was much more than a slogan; it was our governing maxim. It was the foundation of everything we believed about competition. Competitive variables are often unfair. Playing conditions vary greatly from one game to the next and technical performance is unreliable. But no matter how you slice it, at the end of the day, someone wins and someone loses, and winners win. Always.

'Winner' is a label that coaches do not pass around frivolously. It's not about the team that wins one day or the team that wins occasionally or even the team that wins more than it loses. Winners are those athletes and teams that have a mysterious quality surrounding them; that regardless of circumstance, day in and day out, year after year, they find a way to get past all the excuses that they could have used and actually produce results. And because they consistently find a way to produce those results, they develop an aura. Even when

9

things look their bleakest, they still expect to win - and their opponents expect them to win also.

Winners have an aura. You can't play against winners without also playing against their tradition, and although that tradition only exists in the minds of players, it still exists in the minds of players and that makes it too powerful to be overlooked. Winners manage to pull enough rabbits out of enough hats that no one believes a lead is safe against them. That's the thing about winners: Even when their talent falters, luck seems to find them. Time after time, winners produce one miracle after another to the point that they have opponents convinced that they are supposed to win as if it were a divine right. Even when they've played poorly enough to lose, they find a way to win. Because that's what winners do. They win.

In 1999, Fish's freshman year, we finished with a record of 7-12-1. We competed very well; that is to say that we kept a lot of games close, but we were still missing the edge that turns a competitor into a winner. It was especially frustrating because in almost every contest we were radically outworking our opponent, yet we still weren't being rewarded for our effort. It was as if we were on a sled teetering at the top of the hill but we couldn't get that little push we needed to begin our ride. We lacked that mysterious quality that turns a one-goal loss into a one-goal win.

I had to find a way to get my players to compete against each other in training the way our opponents would compete against them during matches. If we were ever going to reach our competitive goals of winning championships, we needed to redefine what qualified as socially acceptable behavior on the training field for every member of our team, and as silly as this may sound, Step One was getting everyone to believe that winning was okay, and permissible, and by any measure a heck of a lot better than losing. We had to give one another permission to win, permission to be happy about it, and even permission to flaunt it.

It was my job to convince the players that we would never win on talent or even on work rate. Just to compete, just to have a chance to win, we had to play on an inconceivable emotional level. And even then we were guaranteed nothing. If a more talented, more athletic team matched us emotionally, then we were probably going to lose. That's why we had to prevent anyone from matching us emotionally.

I spent many team meetings during the 1999 season explaining this concept. In short, our problem was that we were too darn nice. Yes, we wanted to win, but we weren't willing to dive into that gray area where the margin of victory often lies.

Our unwillingness to reject failure at all costs had stunted our ability to win soccer games and we would often leave the field demoralized that we had lost again. More than once after a close loss, I would gather the team and tell them the same thing I'm going to tell you: If you want to win, you have got to change the way you think about competition. You have a comfort zone about competition and until you're ready to abandon it, our results will not change.

In soccer, more than any other team sport, the better team often loses. The team that territorially and statistically dominates a soccer match is guaranteed nothing. Every soccer player can tell you about the time her team out-shot the opponent 18-1 and lost 1-0. Our 1999 team, even lacking in talent, had managed to make a habit of dominating statistically only to lose on the scoreboard. I needed the players to believe that they could have a much more dramatic effect on their results; that they were not at the mercy of the soccer gods. We needed a tiny transition that would take us from thinking that we could win to believing that we *must* win.

Winner was a label we hadn't yet earned, as much as my players would have liked to believe otherwise. I had the unenviable task of convincing them that we were not a group of winners — not yet. And the easiest way for me to get that message across was to bombard them with the simple truth that winners win. Until we could find a way to get the results, we were never to mistake ourselves as winners. Until the results consistently fell into our column, *Winner* was a label we weren't allowed to wear. Winners don't merely come close. Winners win.

Eventually the players decided that they were sick of finishing games as the runner-up. That's when the scales tipped and they began making new decisions about how they would approach competition. That's when they decided that second place just wasn't good enough anymore. And that's when everything changed.

They began applying the principles that would, years later, comprise this book, and almost overnight our results began to improve. They began to believe that winners really do win, consistently, and that you do get to steer your own destiny. They began seeing winning as a choice, a conscious decision they got to make. Once they internalized winning as a choice and losing as the completely unacceptable alternative, we quickly became the dominant team in our conference and one of the best small college soccer teams in the nation.

By the time Fish's senior year rolled around in 2002, I had a team full of players obsessed with winning – not just soccer games – winning everything. We had a competitive drive that few teams could match. We compiled a record of 18-2-1 that year, winning our second consecutive conference and regional championships.

We were not a team full of exceptional players; Fish said that the greatest satisfaction of her career was winning a lot of games against teams that were far more talented. In other words, we won a lot of games we weren't supposed to win. Why did we win? Because we had a team full of winners. And winners win.

The phrase *'Winners win… and winners win'* meant something important in our program, and I hope it will mean as much to you by the time you finish reading. In our context, *Winners win* applied first and foremost to our results on game day. It was unacceptable to hammer our opponent territorially and statistically only to lose on the scoreboard. Playing a great game didn't mean a darn thing if we couldn't also produce the result. The reciprocal also applied. Just because an opponent was better than us or outplaying us did not make it acceptable to be beaten by them. Our expectations of each and every game were very simple: We will find a way to win.

In our program, when we said, *"Winners win,"* what we were really saying is that the result doesn't lie. And when we added the second part, *"…and winners win,"* it meant that there was *always* a way.

This book is about finding a way to get the only acceptable result during a window of limited opportunity, regardless of circumstance.

Winning is not a lottery; it is a series of choices that winners make day after day. It doesn't matter if you're a girl, a boy or a gorilla, you get to decide the price you're willing to pay in the name of victory. If you are willing to pay a high price, believe me, the results will follow.

There's no great mystery to winning. More often than not it's about a series of decisions that winners remember to make. This book is all about those decisions.

PART 2
IT STARTS
WITH YOU

Y ou have a choice. You can choose to dial down your competitive fury because it will help you blend in with the larger crowd, or you can choose to hold yourself to a higher standard and compete like a lunatic because deep down that's who you really are. As long as you keep steering yourself to the middle of the pack, you'll remain wonderfully average. But when you reveal your true competitive colors, the other competitors on your team will gravitate toward you. One player is all it takes. One truly valiant competitor can put her team on a whole new course. I've seen it happen. If winning really does matter to you, fly your flag high and proud. Your teammates who are worth a darn will rally to salute it.

5

It Begins With One

I took the job at Embry-Riddle in February of 1998. We would launch as a varsity program the following August. By February, soccer-playing seniors have already made their college choices. I had virtually no time to recruit, if for no other reason than there weren't any players left to be recruited. In effect, I was taking the university's existing club team and elevating it to varsity status.

I had run two training sessions with the club players. In six months, they would become the varsity team. None of them had ever played a game of college soccer. Some of them had never played a game of club soccer or high school soccer either. Most of them had only played rec soccer and not for any significant length of time. Two of them began playing soccer when they got to college. To summarize, we were in way over our heads.

Florida high school soccer runs through the winter, so I had arrived just in time to catch the tail end of the playoff season. Gainesville Eastside was visiting Daytona Beach to square off with the local powerhouse, Seabreeze High School. The game went into overtime before Seabreeze eventually won in penalty kicks. The result didn't concern me, but what thoroughly consumed me was a player on the Eastside team named Joelle Zucali.

Eastside was outmatched in talent, but Joelle was a total monster. She put that team on her back like nothing I'd ever seen. I had never seen one player work so hard or play with such unmitigated ferocity. She covered a spectacular amount of ground. She didn't seem to play a position; she just went wherever the ball went and threw herself into the fray with utter disregard for her personal safety. She ran; she passed; she dribbled; she shot; and best of all, she knocked opponents on their asses with alarming regularity. She was a one-woman wrecking ball and the reason that Eastside had made it to penalties. I was genuinely inspired to have witnessed such a heroic performance.

As I watched Joelle Zucali, I envisioned that she would come to my university and be the foundation for our team. I hadn't just found a player; I had found our captain. I'd found the warrior personality that would define the culture of our program. She would be our leader, and everyone would gravitate to her standard.

When the game was over and Joelle and her teammates were sitting in the grass changing out of their cleats, I approached her. All I really wanted was to let Joelle know what an honor it had been to watch her play, so I introduced myself and said my piece. I wanted to just turn and walk away and save myself the rejection, but I had to ask if she had already committed to a college. Amazingly, she hadn't. I had just struck gold.

A week later Joelle was visiting our campus. We sat at lunch and I told her that I was going to build my program around her. I told her we would stink at first, but that we would get better with each passing year. Then I made her a promise – a promise I had never made before and have never made since. I promised Joelle that if she came to Embry-Riddle, we would play in a national championship tournament before she graduated. It wasn't the belief I had in myself or my university; it was the immense belief I had in her.

Joelle came on board as my first recruit. Six months later I named this freshman as the lone captain of our program. She was going to be the competitive spirit upon which our program would be built. I wanted her voice to lead us. I wanted her rage to inspire us. I wanted hers to be the standard to which everyone else rose.

As much as I felt that my team full of club players was in over its head as a varsity program, I wondered if I wasn't throwing Joelle into the deep end by naming her as a freshman captain. As it turned out, she may have been better prepared for her assignment than anyone else, including me.

Joelle was mean and nasty and fierce and no one ever hated losing more. She would not accept mediocrity from herself or her teammates, even the ones that were four years her senior. Joelle didn't come to college to win a popularity contest; she came to win soccer games. In no uncertain terms, Joelle Zucali was a winner; and we were on our way.

Joelle taught me that a winning culture starts with one personality. For four years I watched Joelle put our mission ahead of the popularity contest. I watched her drive her teammates forward on pure force of will. Being a champion was very important to Joelle, and she wouldn't allow anything to distract our team from its purpose. And if push came to shove, Joelle wasn't afraid to confront a teammate whose effort was compromising the mission.

If you are serious about winning, then you have to believe that it does begin with one. It begins with one personality that refuses to accept less than excellence; one personality that has the courage to police the standards of the team and confront teammates who aren't living up to those standards. It begins with one personality that has the courage to stand up and say, "This team is about winning championships and you either get on board with that or you pack your bags."

When you were reading about Joelle, maybe there was a part of you thinking, *'Yes! That's how it should be! I want to be like that!'* And then you realize how difficult it's going to be because too many of your teammates won't respond well to that type of leadership. I'm telling you now, if you want to be part of a true winner, you need to choose between your teammates and the mission.

A lot of girls want to win championships, but few have the courage to demand excellence from their teammates. Why? Because girls have a tendency to fire back. When you confront teammates about their effort, there's an excellent chance that they're going to label you something nasty. And that's where you have to decide whether you're going to protect the mission or cave to peer pressure. Ultimately you may have to decide if winning a championship is more important than your relationship with the teammate who regards soccer as a hobby. I'm not saying it's easy. I'm just saying that you won't reach your competitive goals until you have everyone pulling in the same direction. The decision is ultimately yours to make.

Yes, you are only one, but one can be enough. I've seen it happen.

6

You Are the Margin of Victory

"It is not only for what we do that we are held responsible, but also for what we do not do."
- John Baptiste Moliere

Laura DiBernardi will never be inducted into the Embry-Riddle Soccer Hall of Fame. Her jersey will never be retired. She will be remembered by her teammates primarily for being just about the genuinely nicest person you could ever hope to meet. DiBo was known for her kindness, and well, one other thing.

DiBo led a wonderfully unspectacular career. She was steady and dependable and an important piece of the puzzle, but she was not the player fans came to see. She was not the player we counted on to score goals. I don't know how many goals DiBo scored in her four-year career. Five. Maybe six. But sometimes heroes are born because the moment finds them.

In November of 2001, we were playing for a chance to reach our first national championship tournament. All we had to do was win the regional championship match against a team that was much more talented and athletic than we were. Compounding our difficulties, one of our starting forwards received a yellow card ten minutes into the game and I couldn't risk keeping her on the field. If she picked up another card we would have to finish the game with ten players, and there was still a lot of soccer left to play. So I decided to substitute her out of the game and replace her with a freshman who hadn't played very much that year – a girl from New Jersey we all called DiBo.

Fifteen minutes later, our goalkeeper's punt found the head of our center forward, Lisa Lundgren. Lisa's flick-on header at midfield put DiBo in behind the entire defense. From 25 yards, with her first touch, DiBo blasted a sensational volley over the goalkeeper to give us a 1-0 lead. So improbable was this development that in the matter of seconds it took teammates to mob her in celebration, DiBo already had tears cascading down her cheeks. It would be the game's only goal. The most unlikely of players had capitalized on her one chance and made us regional champions. It was Joelle's senior year and I had made good on my promise.

Mathematically speaking, to find the margin of victory, you subtract the loser's score from the winner's score and what you are left with is the margin of victory. By this definition, if a basketball team wins 84-82, then the margin of victory is two points.

But the true margin of victory is something much deeper. It's the sum of all those moments that over the course of an entire game added up to those two points. It's all those rebounds your team collected; all those times you didn't dribble the ball off your shoe or step out of bounds; all those times someone stood in the lane to take a charge; all of those turnovers you forced; and all of those foul shots you made. Add them all together and over the course of forty-eight minutes they added up to two more points than your opponent.

I once heard Colleen Hacker, the renowned sports psychologist for the U.S. Women's National Soccer Team, describe the margin of victory by using the example of two race cars. At the end of a five-hundred mile race, the red car beats the blue car across the finish line by five feet. Somewhere, over the course of five-hundred miles, with cars traveling 200 miles per hour, the driver and crew of the red car managed to scrape out five more feet than the blue car. Those five feet may have come down to something as simple as the red team changing a lug-nut a split second faster than the blue team. We can't pinpoint those five feet, but we know the red car found them somewhere in those 500 miles.

The margin of victory is visible and invisible. It is the sum of all things that appear and do not appear in the box score. It's all the things that did or did not happen and, most importantly, how you influenced them.

Each player holds the margin of victory within her at any and all times. It's not just the great plays that you made; it's also the mistakes that you didn't make. It's how your willingness to hustle back on defense hurried the opponent into a shot she didn't want to take. It's the seemingly harmless turnover you made at midfield that ended up in your own goal. It's the easy chance you missed in the first minute of a game that you go on to lose 1-0. The margin of victory is the sum of all the influence imposed by every player during the course of a game, and ultimately it is found in the final score.

When you accept that *you* are the margin of victory, you understand why it is important to do all things, the big ones and the small ones, to the very best of your ability. You must always chase perfection because you never know when the thing you didn't do becomes the margin of victory for the opponent. And you never know when your opponent is going to give you the chance to become the margin of victory for your team.

The margin of victory is found in the details. Just ask Laura DiBernardi.

If you want to be a winner, you must accept that *you are the margin of victory.*

7

Take Absolute Responsibility

"You can't cheat the game. The game knows."

- Graham Ramsay

One of the legitimate superstars on those Embry-Riddle teams was our goalkeeper, Julie Greenlee. Julie was phenomenal in terms of both ability and fearlessness. She was also a remarkable leader. Moments before we took the field for the 2002 regional championship match, Julie stood up and, to no one in particular, said, "It's time to weigh the bucket." That might not seem very inspiring to you, but to her teammates, Julie had said the magic words.

At Embry-Riddle, when we talked about the importance of our daily preparation, we used a metaphor about drops in a bucket. Here's how it worked:

Our team had a bucket. Every team we'd play against also had its own bucket. And each day some drops went into each team's bucket. When we had a great day of training, a lot of drops poured into our bucket. When we had a mediocre day of training, only a few drops fell into our bucket. Each day we were fighting a battle to put more drops into our bucket than our opponents were putting into theirs. Even when the opponent was invisible, we were still striving to beat her.

As competitors, we have so many variables affecting our lives that it can seem downright overwhelming. There are so many things we have to be accountable for when we are away from our teammates. We have to be responsible for our fitness. We have to be responsible for our strength training. We have to be responsible for our diet. We have to be responsible for rehabilitating our injuries. We have to be responsible for our rest and recovery. And of course we have to be responsible for improving our level of technical competence. With all of these balls in the air, it can be tempting to just walk away. After all, many of these balls are invisible. No one is watching us 24 hours a day. It's much easier to say you went for a thirty-minute run than it is to actually run for thirty minutes. In the short-term, it really is easy to get away with slacking. But as Julie reminded us, eventually there comes a time to weigh those buckets. And at that moment, all those things you haven't done will be exposed.

The one and only thing we have precisely in common with all of our opponents is this: We all have 24 hours in a day. How we choose to spend those 24 hours ultimately determines the weight of our bucket. As a competitor, you need to realize that in the end, when it's time to weigh the bucket, it doesn't really matter to anyone but you.

Yes, your friends care and your parents care and everyone wants to see you do well, but they'll never feel the agony of your failures the way you do. They can't. They haven't made the same physical and emotional investment that you've made. So, while that failure is still haunting you days, weeks or years later, they've long since moved on to other things.

When the game is on the line and your individual battle will determine who wins and who loses, your parents and friends are spectators and nothing more. And as much as they might want to help, on their very best days all they can really be is loud. And loud won't win the game. That's why the responsibility falls to you.

In 2001 we had a talented, freshman midfielder named Nicole Johnston, who we called NJ. NJ showed up unfit for her freshman year and struggled throughout the season. As a matter of fact, NJ wasn't fit enough to finish a single match that year; we had to sub her out of every game. As talented as NJ was, her fitness level kept her from announcing herself as the dominant com-petitor she had the potential to be. She was a piece of our puzzle, but she had a lot more to offer. She finished the season with two goals.

Immediately after her freshman campaign, NJ decided that she was going to be one of our main attractions as a sophomore. She never took a break after our last game that November. To the contrary, she began training harder. She ran her tail off every day and three weeks after her freshman season had ended, the girl who couldn't finish a ninety-minute soccer game completed all 26.2 miles of the Hops Marathon in Tampa.

As a sophomore, NJ showed up as our fittest player. She played virtually every minute of every game, was among our most dominant players, finished fourth in the conference in scoring and was selected to the All-Conference team. And it all started with her decision to take absolute responsibility for her role on our team.

Failing to take absolute responsibility for your training is like habitually failing to brush your teeth before you go to bed. No one is going to hold you accountable for it. If your teeth fall out by the time you're fifty, it's not going to affect *my* life. It might make me cringe a little when we meet, but I'm not going to lose sleep over it the way you will. Brushing your teeth is your responsibility. So is your fitness level. So is your technical improvement. And so is winning.

If it matters to you, then it matters to you and no one else. Excuses are like grapes on a vine waiting to be plucked. Just reach up and grab one. It really doesn't matter to me or anyone else. All I'm going to remember is who won, not why it wasn't you.

Stop leaning on excuses because no one wants to hear them. If you want to be a winner, you need to demand more of yourself. You need to have a higher standard. You need to own the responsibility of steering your ship.

You have 24 hours in a day and so does your opponent. What you choose to do with those 24 hours will determine who has the heavier bucket. The game is ultimately just. It may tease you in the short term, but in the long run the game rewards those who have paid the price. That's how the world turns.

Take absolute and sole responsibility for everything, because it really only matters to you.

8

Find Yourself Guilty

"Peak performance begins with your taking complete responsibility for your life and everything that happens to you."

- Brian Tracy

D o you want to take control of your own destiny right this very second? Sure you do. Who doesn't? Then make this promise to yourself: Regardless of circumstance, *refuse to be a victim!* Don't concede anything to mysterious forces that are beyond your control. The opponent's win had nothing to do with luck; the referee didn't have it out for you; your lack of playing time had nothing to do with your coach's bias. As soon as you begin assigning responsibility for your failures to forces beyond your control, what you're really saying is, *"Look at me! I'm a victim!"*

If there is one thing I cannot tolerate, it's a player who positions herself as a victim. It is a sign of gross immaturity as a player and a person. Victims do not belong in the arena of competition and they certainly do not belong in the setting of a team. If you make a habit of casting yourself as the damsel in distress, it's time to grow the heck up.

The problem is that girls make excellent victims because you are surrounded by rescuers. The world has been very forgiving of your failures. When you fail, you get sad, and because you're a girl, someone wants to run in and give you a hug and make you feel better. So when you fail, you are actually rewarded with human affection. Let me tell you something: That's crap. And the longer you allow the world to distract you from the fact that you didn't get the job done, the deeper the hole you dig yourself. As far as I'm concerned, *victim* is synonymous with *loser*.

Yeah, I get it; you don't want to admit to failure. No one does. It's hard to stand there and say, "I got beat." It's even harder to admit that you're on the bench because your teammate is a better player. But at some point you've got to cowboy up as a competitor and take responsibility for your failures. You've got to hit those failures head on if for no other reason than it will drive you to work harder to avoid them in the future.

One thing humans will never lack is an excuse. It seems every one of our failures as athletes have been heavily influenced by mitigating circumstances such as the referee, the weather, poor coaching, or injury. Or my favorite: bad luck.

Soccer people crack me up. Talk to any soccer coach or player who just lost a close game and 99% of the time that person is going to say, "We should have won. We had three great chances and we just didn't finish. We were just *unlucky*."

It's difficult for coaches and athletes to accept that the team that deserved to win almost always does. Our egos aren't wired for humility. We can't accept that the opponent had more to do with the outcome than destiny did. We prefer to believe that it was all under our control and through bad luck, it was stolen from us.

And just in case we can't find an excuse, fans will line up to give us one. I can't tell you how many times my team has lost a game and a parent has come up afterward to say, "You should have won that one. You were all over that team." Yes, we were all over that team, but they still managed to score one more goal than we did. Whose fault is that?

Well, I can't tell you whose fault it is, but I can tell you whose fault it is not: It is not the fault of the soccer gods. It is not the fault of the referee or the field or the crowd or the weather.

I love it when a team outshoots its opponent 16-2 and loses 2-0, because the next sound you're sure to hear is someone saying, "We deserved to win that game." And as long as that mindset exists, that team will never realize its potential to win.

Taking fourteen more shots than the opponent doesn't mean you deserved to win. Allowing just two shots doesn't mean you deserved to win. It probably indicates that you were the better team, but finishing your chances matters. Goalkeeping matters. The only team that deserved to win was the team that scored the most goals, regardless of every other statistic in the scorebook. The better team and the team that deserved to win are not always one in the same.

If you are going to evolve into a winner, then you need to believe that you are not at the mercy of some capricious destiny. You need to believe that no one can affect your destiny more than you. Most importantly, you need to believe that you do have the power to control that destiny – every last bit of it.

As long as you believe that your destiny is ultimately out of your control, you are granting yourself permission to be a victim. Winners are not victims. Winners steer their own ships.

One of the best decisions I ever made was to develop the habit of tracing every single one of my failures back to me. If my team loses, it's my fault - obviously I failed in some aspect of preparation. If I'm late for work because I got stuck at the railroad crossing, it's my fault because I could have woken up five minutes earlier and been across the tracks before the train ever arrived. If a talented prospect decides to attend another university, it's my fault because I failed somewhere in the recruiting process.

Regardless of circumstance, I'll find a way to trace every failure back to me. I want to believe that I have control of my own life. I want responsibility for the outcome. I refuse to believe that something as haphazard as a cargo train can influence my performance. I refuse to be a victim of a few tons of iron on wheels. And while I may have unrealistic expectations of what I can control, most people completely underestimate how much control they can exert over their own lives. When the Average Jill fails, she can't wait to find an excuse. When you go mining for excuses, what you're really saying is, "I accept that I am a victim being blown along by the winds of happenstance." No thanks. I am my own judge and jury and I will forever choose to find myself guilty.

So, where's the reward?

Once you find yourself guilty, what you're actually saying is, "I am responsible for my own destiny." And because you do not want to be a failure any more than absolutely necessary, that responsibility reinvents itself as accountability. And nothing motivates you more than your own accountability. In the words of the author Erica Jong, "Take your life in your own hands, and what happens? A terrible thing: no one to blame."

When you begin to see your failures as yours and no one else's, you'll be amazed at the lengths you will go to prevent them. And the sum of those lengths is the cornerstone of every winner: work rate. The correlation between work rate and success is paramount. Never will you find one without the other. Work rate is the not-so-secret ingredient in every success formula.

Why then, if we know that work rate is the single most important ingredient to our success, do so many of us refuse to maximize it? That's simple. Work rate involves work, and we'd rather not do work if we can avoid it. And we can avoid it rather easily. All we need is an excuse.

As long as you give yourself excuses to fail, you'll never fully take advantage of your capability for work rate. You always have more to give. Deep down you know you do. You've got to resist the temptation to find the easy way out. You've got to demand more of yourself.

Refuse to be a victim. Believe that you control your own destiny. Do not assign responsibility for your life to happenstance. You have to be stronger than that!

Want to be a winner? Find yourself guilty. Trace every failure back to you and then go to work.

PART 3
CONTROLLING
YOUR DESTINY

The single greatest obstacle to your success is the need to assign blame to someone other than yourself. As long as your reflex reaction is to assign your failures to forces beyond your control, you will never realize your potential. I've seen too many players never reach their goals and it wasn't because they weren't talented enough. This game is *your* thing, so you've got to own every bit of it. Once you accept that this ship is yours to steer, only then will you sail beyond the harbor.

9

Control the Controllables

"Don't hand a monkey a loaded gun and expect him to miss you."

- Scott Arnold

Once you decide that you do have control over your destiny, the next step is exercising that control.

Let me say that there are certainly circumstances over which we have no control. You could be sitting in front of your television one night when a transformer blows and suddenly your neighborhood is without electricity. Nothing you could have done about that and no amount of belief will change it. But if you pay attention during the course of a single day, you'll be amazed at how much you truly do have control over.

Everything in this world falls into three categories: things you can control, things you can influence, and things you have no control over whatsoever. One of the mantras of our soccer program was that we were going to control everything we had the power to control, influence everything we had the power to influence, and not worry about the rest.

At the beginning of the season I had my team make three lists: The things we could control completely, the things we could influence, and the things we had no control over whatsoever.

The list of things we could not control typically contained things like the weather, the referee's whistle (once it has blown), the condition of an opponent's field, the natural ability of our opponent, and the actions of the opponent's fans.

We believed we could influence the referee's attitude towards us and thus, some of his decisions, the opponent's decisions on the ball, the spirit of the opponent, and the spirit of the opponent's fans.

The things we had complete control over included our preparation, our emotional readiness, our attitude, our aggression, our courage, our confidence, our pride, our work-rate, our fitness level, our willingness to take physical risks, our team tactics, our communication, clock management, hunting rebounds and our decisions on the ball.

Later we will review how to cope with the things we cannot control, but for now, let's look at all of the things we can control and can influence. When you look at those two lists, do you see an opportunity to dominate?

I believe we can win nearly every game if we can win those two categories. Even if we concede every item on the out-of-our-control list to our opponent including speed and talent, there is still ample opportunity for us to find a way to win. But to completely concede one category and still win, we've got to be control freaks. We need to recognize all of those moments when we have the opportunity to exert control or influence and we need to act on them. They comprise our window of opportunity.

As an athlete, you have a great deal of control over the portion of your day or your week not spent with your team. Even with commitments of school and work, there is always time to be found if you choose to find it. In that time you can choose to get fitter; you can choose to get in the weight room; you can choose to work on your technical ability. Or you can choose not to do any of those things. If you want to narrow the talent gap, take control of the things you can control – *all of them*. Be great at the things the opponent isn't even calculating into the equation. That's how winners level the playing field. That's how a player like Tiffany Roberts gets to be an Olympic gold medalist. She played the game on her terms, excelling at the things she could control. Soccer isn't just about the magic inside a player's shoes. Talent is just one of an endless array of variables. Roberts was good with her feet, but she made herself invaluable with the things that she had control over – like her head and her heart and her willingness to use her speed to her advantage.

Elizabeth Fisher was remarkable at controlling the controllables. She had to be. Why? Because she wasn't the world's greatest soccer player. Fish knew that if she wanted to get on the field, she needed to make up for a lack of talent. How did she know that? Because I told her. At the start of every preseason I tried to train someone to take her place. I was certain that we needed a more talented player in her position as a central defender. Over the course of four years, I tried an array of more talented players in her spot, at least a half-dozen, but none could win the position from her.

Can you imagine what it was like to be Elizabeth Fisher? For four years Fish had to put up with a coach that was actively trying to give away her spot! And for four years she refused to let me give that spot away. She did that by controlling everything she had the power to control.

In a strange sense, Fish had an advantage. She had something to prove each and every time she went to training. She knew that if she gave me an excuse, I was going to put her on the bench. Every day she had a reason to be motivated. She knew she had to perform every single day. And I'll be darned if she didn't do exactly that.

Fish made herself indispensable with the things she could control. She was emotionally primed every time she set foot on the field. She never had a flat training session – *not once!* She always reported to preseason as one of our fittest players. No one worked harder. She never jogged when she could sprint, never walked when she could run. She was fiercely competitive and demanding of her teammates. She was very vocal, constantly barking out instructions to her teammates and holding them accountable. Above all else, Fish chose courage.

Fish wasn't a big girl, but she threw her body around with total disregard for personal safety. There wasn't a tackle she wouldn't dive into or a header she wouldn't challenge. And as much as I tried, I could never make one of those more talented players take the same physical risks. They would never affect the game the way Fish did. Fish's willingness to put herself in harm's way was critical in helping us win a lot of soccer games.

Fish chose to make the most of what she had. She refused to let talent be the decisive factor in her playing time. She chose to exercise control and left nothing to chance. Every day she played the game with a do-or-die freedom. That's why she was a four-year starter in our program.

It's not always easy to control all your controllables, even when you recognize the moment. Sometimes it takes a great deal of courage to go up and win a header or to stand in the lane and take a charge or to let that inside fastball pop you in the arm. But make no mistake – you get to choose whether or not you are going to do any of those things. You can choose courage just as easily as you can choose an easier path. But in any sport, those opportunities to change a game rarely happen twice. Once you make your choice, you've got to live with it.

I am a fanatic about hunting rebounds. In a game of soccer, which can get mired down in the give and take of possession changes, sometimes all it takes is one ambitious player sniffing for a rebound to win the game.

During the 2002 season our team scored five rebound goals in the final five minutes of a game or in sudden-death overtime. Four of those goals were game-winners while one tied a game that we went on to win in overtime. One of those rebound goals won us a championship.

Hunting rebounds requires not one iota of talent. It is something we have complete control over. All it takes is recognition and running. That's it! In soccer, almost never can you do less and get rewarded for it. When a teammate was getting ready to shoot, all we had to do was run at the goalkeeper. Recognize and run. And nearly 100% of the time the opponents won't hunt for those same rebounds because they are too busy waiting to see if the goalkeeper will make the save.

Sometimes there was a rebound, sometimes there wasn't. But when there was, we wanted to cash in. It was something we could control and that meant we needed to own it. Our willingness to control rebound hunting won twenty-five percent of our games and one championship for us!

If you don't control the controllables, you're just playing a lottery, and no one consistently wins the lottery. If you can control it, you've got to own it, because you never know when the margin of victory is going to reveal itself.

Want to be a winner? Start by controlling the controllables.

10

The Talent Gap

"Gentlemen, you are not talented enough to win on talent alone."
- Herb Brooks, Head Coach, 1980 U.S. Hockey Team

In any endeavor, whether it is sports or business or arts and crafts, a hierarchy exists. There is the person or team that is Best, and then there is everyone else. And the difference between the top dog and all the other dogs that are chasing him is what we will call the talent gap.

As an athlete, you are evaluated in four areas: technical ability, physical ability, tactical ability, and psychological strength. Best is the one who has managed to embody the most powerful combination of these elements. Let's refer to that combination as *talent*.

As long as Best and Second Best travel parallel paths, Second Best will never be able to catch or overtake Best. Somehow Second Best has to find a way to close that talent gap to put herself within striking distance of Best. And a lot of times, Best simply has and always will have more natural ability than Second Best. The challenge for Second Best is to do the things that Best may not always do and to perfect areas where Best is content to remain imperfect. The challenge for Second Best is to maximize everything Second Best has the power to maximize.

If you are the best in the world at what you do, this book definitely is not for you. This book is intended for everyone who is chasing you. This book is for all of us who want what you have and are willing to do what's necessary to take it away.

You see, you may always be more gifted than me. You may always be stronger and faster. You may always be able to do more with a ball or a stick or a racket. Over the long haul, you may just be flat-out better than me. But I might not have to worry about the long haul. Chances are that I do not have to beat you every day of the year. Chances are I only have to beat you once.

I have enough drive to get me close. I have enough ability and determination to put me in a position to compete with you. And on that day when we compete, I hope to have my very best day — and I hope that you have something slightly less. And by the time you realized what happened, it may be too late, because in sports, once is often enough.

Beware of the enemy you cannot see. Beware of me because I am chasing you. Every day I'm closing the talent gap a little bit more. The advantage you have over me in body I can surpass with power of mind. I'm going to pay attention to the details and I'm going to put myself in the very best position to win. And on the day you forget what it means to you, I'll be there to capitalize.

11

Give Yourself a Chance to Be Lucky

"The harder I work, the luckier I get."
- Samuel Goldwyn

Super Bowl Twenty Seven. Dallas Cowboys linebacker Leon Lett recovers a Buffalo Bills fumble and is on his way into the endzone for an easy touchdown. Lett is unaware that Bills' receiver Don Bebe has been at a full sprint from midfield and is rapidly closing ground. It shouldn't have mattered. Even though Bebe was much faster than Lett, Lett's head-start was more than enough to guarantee the Cowboys a touchdown... provided Lett kept running.

Instead of hustling in for the touchdown, Lett eased up and began showboating over the final ten yards. Just before Lett crossed into the endzone, Bebe flew in and knocked the ball from Lett's hands. The ball skipped through the endzone and out of bounds. Instead of six more points for Dallas, it was ruled a touchback and Buffalo got the ball at its own twenty-yard line.

In his book *Swim With The Sharks Without Being Eaten Alive*, Harvey McKay tells readers to 'Be #2.' What he means is, if you can't be number one, do everything in your power to position yourself as number two, and not number three, four, or five. Eventually the pack-leader will goof. And when she does, you want to make sure it's you and not someone else who is the beneficiary. In short, what McKay is saying is, *give yourself a chance to be lucky.*

Bebe's heroics did nothing to change the outcome. The Cowboys already had an insurmountable lead. The result was already decided, which makes Bebe's dash even more heroic. I can't think of another moment in sports that illustrates the principles of winning better than the Leon Lett – Don Bebe encounter. Lett violated nearly all the principles in this book while Bebe showcased them.

In the grand scheme of things, Bebe really had no business working that hard to catch up to Lett. There was no possible way he was going to catch the Cowboy. The only way that Bebe's work would have made any difference was if he got very, very lucky. He needed Lett to do something foolish to even have a chance at affecting the play.

Did Bebe get lucky? Absolutely. Lett gave away control of something of which he had total control – how hard he chose to run – but that did not make Bebe lucky. Lett only gave Bebe the opportunity to be lucky. If Bebe doesn't run so hard to recover and Lett still showboats, there is no memorable play. There is only Lett scoring a touchdown and no one would have been the wiser.

Bebe gave himself a chance to be lucky by controlling the one thing he could control at that moment – his own work rate. He wouldn't have been able to capitalize if he didn't do the work that most people would not have seen the point in doing. And because the gods of sport occasionally smile down upon us, Bebe was rewarded with some very good luck.

Winners know the importance of stacking the deck. They take nothing for granted. They are always thinking about positioning themselves for the best possible outcome. They know that all teammates and opponents are human, and that all humans are fallible. Winners assume that if they do the right things, good luck will follow. Winners control what they can and they put themselves into position to be lucky.

Game Six of the 1980 World Series. With one out in the ninth inning, Phillies' reliever Tug McGraw is pitching to Kansas City Royals' batter Frank White. Philadelphia's Veterans Stadium is buzzing with anticipation. The Phillies are two outs away from their first World Series championship. White hits a lazy pop fly into foul territory along the first base line. Phillies' catcher Bob Boone drifts underneath it, putting himself in position to make a routine catch. But Boone misjudges the ball. He starts to backpedal frantically. He jabs his mitt out to make the catch. The ball pops out of Boone's mitt and heads towards the ground, taking Philadelphia's championship hopes with it.

But just inches before the ball reaches the ground, Phillie's first baseman, Pete Rose, stabs out his glove and snatches it to record the out. Tug McGraw strikes out the next batter and Philadelphia wins the World Series.

Were Rose and the Phillies lucky? Somewhat. There were many different paths that ball could have taken once it left Boone's mitt, and most of them wouldn't have given Rose a chance to make that catch. But it didn't take those paths. It only took one path. And because Pete Rose took nothing for granted and controlled all that he could, when the opportunity for good luck presented itself, he was able to capitalize. None of which would have happened if Rose didn't assume that he might be able to make a difference by putting himself so close to Boone. Winners do the things that cultivate good luck, *just in case.*

How do you cultivate good luck? Simple. You cultivate good luck by do- ing the very best you can regardless of circumstance. When Bebe started his dash to catch Lett, maybe the governing thought in his head was as simple as, *'Is there something better I can be doing right now?'* Maybe Bebe asked himself that question, answered no, then took off running. By constantly putting yourself in the best possible position, even if that position is as #2, you give yourself a chance to be lucky.

Here's a story about some players that totally violated this principle and paid the price.

One of the steadfast rules on my team is that 'On-time means early.' I'm a nut about punctuality and the players have always known this. Tardiness always equates to some type of punishment, usually a one-game suspension.

In 2002 we had a 7 A.M. departure for a game in Miami. This was an important game. If we lost, we would be eliminated from winning the conference title.

One of the strengths of our team was that we had an exceptional goalkeeper. Because she was so good at her job, our second-string goalkeeper had very few opportunities to play and our third-string goalkeeper never had the opportunity.

At 7 A.M. on this very important day, seven of my players still weren't on the bus, including our All-American goalkeeper. Finally, the second-string goalkeeper would get her chance to start. Except she wasn't there either. That meant the duty fell to the third-string goalkeeper. Guess who else wasn't on the bus. All three of our goalkeepers, as well as a starting central defender, central midfielder, outside midfielder, and forward had all missed the departure time! I suspended them all for that game.

We had reserves for all of the field-players, but we were out of goalkeepers. I had a three-hour bus ride to figure a solution. As our bus rolled down the interstate, I decided to promote our equipment manager, Lisa Bush, to goalkeeper. Bushy was a college senior who had played goalkeeper in high school. I kept her name on our roster just in case a real emergency came up. One had.

All that either of the reserve goalkeepers had to do to become a starter that day was to show up on time. If either one of them had better managed something she had complete control over – namely her alarm clock – she would have been our starting goalkeeper. Instead, neither of those players gave themselves a chance to be lucky. When the number one goalkeeper finally goofed, neither of her back-ups was in a position to capitalize.

We went on to win that game, thanks in large part to our equipment manager who made some excellent saves early in the match. And, as fate would have it, we went on to win our second consecutive conference championship.

The problem with positioning yourself for luck is that it requires patience, discipline, and the unwavering belief that if you keep doing the right things, eventually you will be rewarded for it. Winners have that unwavering belief. They believe that the game is ultimately just. That's why they continually do the right things. That's why they continually win.

Day after day after day our back-up goalkeepers had arrived on time but were never rewarded for it because the starting goalkeeper had also always been on time. On the one day she wasn't, no one was there to pick up the crumbs. The back-ups had forgotten what it was worth to them to show up on time. They gave away a piece of control. They didn't give themselves a chance to be lucky. Can you imagine how foolish they felt watching that game?

Regardless of the sport, most coaches will tell you that games are lost more than they are won. In addition to giving yourself a chance to win, you've also got to give your opponent a chance to lose. You've got to give the opponent the opportunity to be a fallible human being.

A piece of advice you'll hear baseball coaches espouse from Little League to the pros is 'Put the ball in play.' You won't hear them say, "Go hit a home run," or "Go hit a double." But you'll always hear them saying "Put the ball in play." Why? Because the absolute worst thing you can do as a batter is strike out. When you strike out, you take away the opportunity for your opponent to mishandle a ground ball or to misfire on the throw to first base. You take away the opportunity for a crazy bounce or a collision between two outfielders. In short, you take away your chance to be lucky. To get to first base, you need to put the ball on the field of play.

In tennis and volleyball you've got to get your serve in bounds or the opponent never gets the chance to make a mistake. In basketball you've got to drive the lane to give the opponent a chance to foul you. Regardless of the sport, you've got to give the opponent a chance to screw up or you are doing her job for her.

Soccer coaches know how important it is for players to get their shots on goal. We constantly tell our players to make the goalie make a save. If you hit the ball over or wide of the goal, you don't force the goalkeeper into performing. You don't let her humanness reveal itself. When you shoot off target, you let the goalkeeper off the hook. If however, you do get your shot on frame, a world of possibilities unfolds including goalkeeper error and rebound opportunities.

In the chapter on Controlling the Controllables, we briefly discussed the value of rebounds in soccer. The problem with hunting rebounds is that you are counting on your opponent to be imperfect. If she's not, your work goes unrewarded. It takes a winner's unwavering belief to continually do work that will go unrewarded the vast majority of the time. You may hunt rebounds ninety-nine times and none will appear. But if you don't hunt on that one hundredth shot, you can bet that's when a rebound will materialize.

Earlier I mentioned our central midfielder NJ. In 2002, NJ became a fanatical hunter of rebounds. She scored several rebound goals during the regular season, including one game-winner in sudden death overtime.

In the regional championship match, with the scored tied 1-1 late in the second half, there was a scramble in the opponent's goal box. Eventually the ball bounced up to Denise Brolly at the penalty spot. Denise did a quick pivot then launched a bicycle kick at the goal. The goalkeeper dove to make the save, but she didn't hang on to the ball. NJ was first to the rebound and stuffed it into the net. The goal that won us that championship was neither artistic nor powerful. It required minimal technical ability. The most important goal of the season was scored from two yards off the goal-line.

Was NJ's goal lucky? Let's see.

I've watched the video of that goal many times. When Denise jumps into the air to take her shot, there are four opposing players between NJ and the goal; four opponents that would have had a head start on NJ if everyone had left at the same time. Any one of them would have beaten NJ to the ball if they all started running before the ball bounced out of the goalkeeper's hands.

But as soon as Denise committed to taking her shot, NJ sprinted straight at the goal and straight past all four of those opposing players. While the four opponents were mesmerized by the bicycle kick, NJ was giving herself the best possible chance to be lucky. Five players had a chance to be first to that rebound, but only one put herself in position to be that player. Thankfully she was the one player who played for our team.

So again, were we lucky? In a sense, yes. The goalkeeper probably should have caught that ball cleanly even though she had to dive for it. We were lucky that the opportunity presented itself. But we never would have been able to capitalize if NJ hadn't made the decision to a hunt for a rebound that might never have materialized. If NJ doesn't hunt for that rebound, the play becomes inconsequential.

Luck happens when preparation meets opportunity. NJ was prepared to hunt rebounds. The goalkeeper gave her an opportunity to be rewarded for it. And our opponent will forever believe that we were lucky to win that game.

As for NJ, she got to be a hero to her teammates and her university in front of the biggest crowd ever to see a game in our stadium. Isn't that worth running twelve yards?

Sports are rife with mind-numbing moments where the unthinkable materializes right in front of your eyes. One of the greatest gifts you can give yourself as an athlete is to assume that one of those moments is always close at hand. You have to assume the opponent is going to make a mistake. You assume that a rebound will appear so you go looking for it. You assume that ball will be mishandled by the shortstop so you sprint all the way to first base. You do whatever you can to put yourself in the very best position.

Winners cultivate their own luck. If you want to consistently win, you've got to consistently give yourself a chance to be lucky. In the end you've got to ask yourself, is there something better for me to be doing right now? If the answer is no, go looking for luck.

12

Be Paranoid

"Just because you're paranoid, don't mean they're not after you".

- Kurt Cobain

D id you ever see reruns of the old Batman series and wonder why the Penguin never just picked up a gun and shot Batman and Robin? The Penguin, Joker, Riddler and Catwoman all had ample chances to eliminate their nemesis. They all had the Dynamic Duo incapacitated and dead to rights. But instead of getting the job done the easy way, they would erect some complex, suspense-inducing death machine, like a conveyor belt headed for a buzz saw, and inevitably Batman and Robin would free themselves in the nick of time and then go on to capture the bad guys and save Gotham City.

Why did those villains fail? Simple. They were overconfident. More precisely, they weren't paranoid.

Not familiar with that show? Let's try a moment from sports that you may remember:

July 10, 2011. Team USA faced off against Brazil in the quarterfinal of the Women's World Cup. Brazil was clinging to a 2-1 lead very late into the second overtime. With merely seconds to go and the Americans playing a man down,

Brazilian striker Cristiane had the ball out on the wing, deep in U.S. territory. To secure the victory, all Cristiane had to do was hold the ball down in the corner and time would have expired. Instead, she decided to square up to the goal and thread a difficult pass between a pair of American defenders. Her pass was deflected away. Seventeen seconds later, Abby Wambach headed the ball into the Brazilian goal, the game was tied, and the U.S. went on to win in penalty kicks.

After the match, Wambach's header was all anyone in America was talking about. But it was Cristiane's mistake that set the whole thing in motion.

All Cristiane had to do was stand on the ball near the corner flag and Brazil would have eliminated the Americans and advanced to the semifinals. But instead of showcasing a healthy dose of paranoia, she decided to go freelancing and the result was a Brazilian disaster.

The miraculous American comeback was one of those high-profile moments where the gods of sport pull the rug out from under someone. Because it was so high-profile, we might mistake it as an aberration; something that could only happen once in a lifetime. And when we make that mistake, we're begging history to repeat itself.

Paranoia is classified as an irrational fear, but in sports, there is nothing irrational about it. Why? Because on game day, the bogeyman really is out to get you. So while the opponent is giving herself a chance to be lucky, you had better be countering it with extreme paranoia.

The 2006 Winter Olympics introduced us to an American snowboarder who blew her gold medal and immediately began drawing comparisons to Leon Lett.

Lindsey Jacobellis had the gold medal for Snowboard Cross practically sewn up as she approached the second to last jump of the final run. A collision amongst her three other competitors had given Jacobellis a massive lead. All Jacobellis had to do was stay upright and the first gold medal in the history of Snowboard Cross was hers.

Instead of merely taking the jump with a healthy dose of winner's paranoia, Jacobellis got careless. She spiced up her final jump with huge air, threw in a trick, and promptly crashed the landing. Switzerland's Tanja Frieden, who was practically in another zip code from the initial crash, zipped by Jacobellis to win the gold.

Jacobellis, like Leon Lett and Cristiane, violated two of the most important principles of winning. She gave away control of something she had total control over. And she wasn't paranoid.

The examples of Lett and Jacobellis are extreme. Hopefully you will never be bitten quite so hard by such a large bug of carelessness, but Cristiane's blunder serves as a shining reminder about how a momentary lack of concentration can cause a great day to quickly unravel.

Winners know that no lead is invincible. They have a respect for the game and for the gods and they treat them both with due reverence. Any opponent can hurt you if you give her the chance. You've got to respect what she can do to you and you've got to do everything in your power to eliminate that possibility – and that includes making a steadfast commitment to vaporizing her fighting spirit.

Most players with a lead gravitate toward complacency. Winners, on the other hand, gravitate toward bloodlust. They see the job through to the very end without mercy or remorse. They'll happily beat a dead horse just to make it deader.

Anyone can say, "I hate to lose." All athletes would like to believe that about themselves, but very few genuinely regard losing as a humiliating catastrophe to be avoided at all costs. Winners have this beautiful paranoia that won't let them take their foot off the gas regardless of the score. They love winning, *but they are utterly obsessed about not losing.* They refuse to give the opponent a chance to hurt them. They are the ones who will gladly do the dirty work that others are not willing to do. They refuse to accept defeat as an option. And I cannot possibly have enough of those players on my team.

It wasn't until Fish's junior year that our program hit its stride and became a legitimate contender to win the regional championship tournament. The winner of that tournament would advance to the national championship tournament, and that was our ultimate goal.

Fish had endured a 7-12-2 season as a freshman and a 10-7-1 season as a sophomore. We had played in only one playoff game. It was during her sophomore year and we blew a 1-0 lead late in the second half to lose 2-1. Fish was tired of watching other teams celebrate and she had learned a hard lesson about getting comfortable with a lead.

Now, during her junior year, we had reached the regional championship match and Laura DiBernardi's remarkable volley had given us a 1-0 lead in the 25th minute, and we would have to make it stand up for another 65.

With thirty minutes left in the match, Fish's voice became the driving voice of our team. From her position at central defender, she shouted, "Only 30 more minutes! What's it worth to you!" Then she shouted the same thing when there were 29 minutes left. And 28. And so on.

Fish refused to let her teammates lose focus. Her best friend and roommate, Michelle 'Mac' McCoy, was one of our central midfielders. Whenever it looked like Mac was getting winded, Fish shouted at her, "You're not tired, Mac! Get your ass back here!"

Fish was in this intense mental zone fueled by a beautiful paranoia, demanding the best from her teammates, driving them to the finish line. If someone was walking, Fish got her to jog. If she was jogging, Fish got her to run. Elizabeth Fisher was not going to let anyone forget about the importance of finishing the job. She wouldn't allow anyone to switch off, not for a second.

Fittingly, the game ended when Fish booted a clearance over the opponent's line of defenders and into a deserted corner of the field as time expired. We had beaten a more talented team and won our first championship, and Fish's paranoia was a major reason for the result.

You have to be paranoid until the final out or the final whistle or the final hole. Winning is a fickle, fickle thing. As soon as it bores you, I promise, it will go away. Don't celebrate or relax one second before the game is over. Take nothing for granted because the gods of sport are always on the lookout for the butt of their next practical joke. As soon as you take your foot off the gas, you volunteer as a candidate. That's why you don't take your foot off the gas until the game is over.

Take nothing for granted. Once you've seen a miracle, you fear the miracle. Beware of the opponent who is giving herself a chance to be lucky. Stay paranoid. Finish your job. Relax when the game is over and not a second before.

13

Charity Matters

"Even mighty rivers can run dry."

- Anonymous

et's say that on one beautiful night you've mastered all of these principles
and given yourself a chance to win. There is still one fabulous way to shoot
yourself in the foot, and that's by failing to execute those athletic maneuvers
that you are clearly capable of executing. It's not enough to give yourself a
chance to be lucky if you don't actually cash in when luck appears. When the
gods of sport lead you to water, you've got to drink.

No coach expects you to perform miracles with the ball. We understand
that there's a limit to each player's abilities. What coaches do expect is that you
do the things we know you can do. As basketball coaches are fond of saying,
"You've got to make your lay-ups."

You can't expect to beat an opponent by constantly letting her off the hook.
When opportunities present themselves, you simply must capitalize. A basketball team cannot expect to win if it shoots thirteen percent from the foul-line.
A tennis player can't win if she constantly double-faults her serves. Soccer
teams cannot miss their sitters from ten yards and expect to win the game.

In soccer, if your team has made the talent gap negligible, you'll probably have enough chances to win the game. The other team may score two goals and win 2-0, but your team will probably have three or more good chances. When those chances appear, they've got to end up in the net. The gods are offended when you don't take their charity. Pretty soon they stop offering it.

You've got to execute the things you are capable of executing. You've got to make your lay-ups. When the game gives you a chance to exert total control, you've got to perform. To be a winner, you've got to cash in on the freebies.

14

Earmuffs

"Sticks and stones may break my bones..."
- Unknown

One of the major advantages we enjoyed at Embry-Riddle was a rowdy fan base that turned out in droves to support our women's soccer team. Your home field should be a tough place for the opponent to play, and at Embry-Riddle, it was.

Every rowdy fan knows the one thing that every player should know: As soon as you talk back to the fans, they've got you. They know it and they'll use it. At Embry-Riddle, our fans looked forward to the challenge of getting an opposing player to snap back at them. Once a player did that, she was toast. It didn't matter what she said. It didn't matter what gesture she made. The instant she let the fans know that she heard them, they rode her relentlessly.

In the 2004 Regional Tournament semi-final, two of our opponent's best players asked to be substituted out of the game about midway through the first half. Our fans had gotten so deep into their heads that they completely lost the plot before the game was thirty minutes old. They weren't enjoying the event.

They just wanted it to be over. When they were subbed off, they went back behind their bench and cried.

We went on to win that game by a score of 2-0, partly due to the fact that some of our opponent's best players weren't on the field for long stretches at a time. They couldn't play soccer because they were too busy getting counseling.

Winners know that part of a great atmosphere is the fan base, regardless of whether that fan base is on your side. It's a lot more fun to play in front of a lot of hostile fans than in front of a lot of empty seats.

When you understand that the rules of society are different inside the arena of competition, it allows you to enjoy the whole of the event. It lets you enjoy the opponent who is trying to destroy you. It lets you enjoy the fans who are trying to rattle you. It lets you enjoy all those physical battles instead of taking them as personal affronts. Winners enjoy the intensity of the event because they know the intensity makes it worthwhile. The opponent and all the fans, friendly and hostile, contribute to that intensity.

There's an old story about Pete Rose playing for the Cincinnati Reds in the sixth game of 1975 World Series against the Boston Red Sox in Fenway Park. The story goes like this: Rose comes to bat in the tenth inning. Forty thousand Red Sox fans are booing him, hissing him, taunting him, and doing everything in their power to make sure Rose knows that everyone in the ballpark wants him to strike out. Rose turns to Red Sox catcher Carlton Fisk, smiles and says, "Isn't this great?"

Isn't this great?

Can you imagine? In a moment when his bat seemed to be carrying the weight of the world, Pete Rose wasn't overwhelmed by the enormity of the event; he was bathing in it!

We played in certain venues where the fans were more than obnoxious; they were downright vulgar. I told my players to prepare themselves to be called a lot of horrible things. I always told that Pete Rose story before we went into those hostile venues. And I reminded them of the fabulous words of Eleanor Roosevelt who said, "No one can make you feel inferior without your permission."

There is a physical boundary between the fans and the field, and only their voices can cross that boundary. And I've never seen a voice kick a ball. Regardless of what those fans say, they are still only words. You need to understand that those words are not responsible for how you respond to them. You are the only one responsible for your response. You can't control the taunts, but you can certainly control your response. And you must. So when an opposing fan starts to target you, don't take the bait! Just put on your earmuffs and carry on with the game.

When you mature into a competitor who genuinely appreciates the whole of the event the way Pete Rose did, it becomes much easier to control your emotions during the course of the event. It lets you reposition those fans from enemies to allies, because you understand that they are serving to make the event more memorable. Appreciate those fans. And if you can't manage to do that, then at the very least, keep your lip buttoned.

Winners don't talk back to the crowd!

15

Never Retaliate

"He who angers you conquers you."
- Elizabeth Kenny

This was a common event during Joelle Zucali's time in our program:

As a wing midfielder, Joelle would be running down the field in accordance with the flow of play while the ball was all the way on the opposite side of the field. An opponent would be running right behind her. When the opponent eventually caught up, she would swat Joelle's legs out from underneath her. One of the officials would catch the infraction. We would be awarded a free kick and the opponent was usually yellow-carded.

After the game I would stop at the bleachers and say hello to Joelle's mom. She would ask me if I saw that girl kick 'my Joelle.' I would say, "Mrs. Zucali, I'm not exactly sure why that girl kicked your daughter, but I'm pretty sure Joelle deserved it."

Mrs. Zucali saw her daughter as an angel, but I knew better. Joelle had done something to set off her opponent. It was her signature.

Someday you're going to have to play against an opponent like Joelle. If you are not prepared, what you are in for that day is an epic learning experience.

Joelle played right up against the rules of the game, always testing the referee's boundaries. She was a master of manipulation. She didn't wait for the opponent to push her buttons. Joelle never put herself in a situation where she was the one retaliating. Instead, she made a point of putting her opponent in that position as quickly as possible. The moment the opponent started focusing on revenge, Joelle's work was nearly done because the opponent was no longer focusing on winning the game. Joelle understood this and she used it to her advantage game after game after game.

One of the golden rules of any contact sport is this: *Don't retaliate because the referee always catches the second foul.* The ref may miss the first foul, but the clamor will draw his attention and he'll be looking straight at the player who retaliates.

In the 2006 World Cup final, French soccer star Zinedine Zidane was ejected for head-butting Italian defender Marco Materazzi. Materazzi spent the game taunting Zidane until Zidane finally snapped. In the world's single-most important game, the French team had lost the services of the tournament's best player because he had lost his temper and retaliated.

I am severely disappointed whenever my team ends up retaliating. It's an unacceptable circumstance because it means that we weren't the physical and emotional aggressor to begin with. If we had taken the field as the aggressors, it would be the other team retaliating against us. We would be in their heads instead of the other way around. When you find yourself retaliating, you are playing a game of catch-up that you will never win. And it's your own darn fault.

The most aggravating player to coach is the one who doesn't take the field with emotional urgency and then ends up in a frenzy because a clever opponent like Joelle has gotten into her head. Why did it take an opponent to bring out your emotional fury? Why didn't you start the game in that frame of mind? If you had, you could have played the game on your terms. Your emotion would have been an ally instead of a liability.

One of the remarkable characteristics about the teams I coached from 2000-2004 is that we never were among the league leaders in fouls or cards. In most games, the opponent out-fouled us. That wasn't because we lacked aggression; it's because we oozed it. We shot out of the gates with so much aggression that opponents typically ended up fouling us out of frustration. We utilized every square inch of the rulebook from the outset and that made us a very aggravating team to deal with.

The world is full of clever players who thrive on baiting their opponents. You've got to understand that they are out there and if you don't respond to them correctly, your head is going to be everywhere but in the game. Once you lose the plot, you are on the fast-track to self-destruction and you're probably going to take your team down with you.

When the urge to retaliate finds you, and at some point it will, you've got to gather your wits quickly enough to ask yourself: *What am I trying to accomplish right now?* The answer is almost always that you want to make yourself feel better. That's not a good enough reason to risk crippling your team.

No one wants to feel victimized. It's understandable to want to defend your body and your pride, but don't do it in a way that might jeopardize your team. If an opponent baits you into a situation where you physically retaliate, there's an excellent chance that you are going to be ejected from the game, and that's unacceptable.

If you are one of those players that can let verbal and physical attacks roll off you, fantastic! For the rest of us, we've got to take a deep breath and remember the big picture – winning the game.

Contact sports offer ample opportunities to avenge yourself. You'll get your chance to sit that girl down. When you get your chance, do it hard and clean and with conviction. Do it in such a way that she won't want to play that private little game anymore. Send your message and move on. Don't spend the entire match playing a game of one-up. When you start doing that, you're no good to your team any more. When revenge drives you, you are a liability. You will end up hurting your team to make yourself feel better and that's just selfish.

Never punish your team to make yourself feel better. Your teammates have worked too hard to have you throw it away on their behalf. I don't care how bad it hurt or how embarrassing it is – do not retaliate! There are bigger fish to fry. You've got to remember that no matter how angry you become.

Under the most trying of circumstances, winners still remember not to retaliate.

16

The Uncontrollables – You Still Have a Choice

"When you're going through hell, keep going."
                                        - Winston Churchill

There are some variables which are beyond your influence. There aren't many, but there are definitely a few. These are the *uncontrollables* and you need to know how to handle them.

Winners realize that when something is beyond their influence, they cannot affect it. If a winner can't affect it, she won't waste time or energy worrying about it. Of all those variables that are beyond our influence, the one we need to recognize as non-alterable and insignificant is the past. I don't care how good you are, no one has enough talent to change history.

Do you put your head down and mope after you make a mistake? Do you flail your arms in the air when a teammate makes a mistake because of how her imperfection has totally ruined the universe's opportunity to serve you? If you do, take this advice: Stop with the drama and get on with the game. Mistakes happen. They happen all the time.

The ball rolls through your legs at short-stop. You double fault your service. You air-ball your free throw. Your putt sails by the cup, off the green, and into the pond. The referee makes a horrendous call. A teammate gets ejected. A teammate gets injured. The opponent scores. You accidentally kick the ball into your own net. Disasters, each and every one of them. No way around it. But they are disasters that every team must face from time to time. Once those moments occur, you can't get them back. Accept it.

No one, not even the galaxy's mightiest winner, can change the past. You can, however, respond to it. As a matter of fact, that's all you can do. How you respond to these disasters is a conscious choice that you get to make. And no matter how many circumstances conspire against you, no matter how badly the game turns on you, no matter how badly or blatantly your team just got hosed, you still and always will have a choice as to how you will respond. Remember that.

One of my favorite traditions in our program was started by my assistant coach, Mike Cole, during the 2000 season. Before each game we would send our captains out for the coin flip. They would return and tell us which end of the field we were defending. On most days, the coin toss is pretty insignificant. But on certain days, like when it's especially windy, there's an end of the field we would prefer to defend first. Unfortunately, once the coin goes into the air, there's not a darn thing we can do to affect our chances.

Regardless of the news our captains brought back, Mike's response was always a booming shout of, "Just what we wanted!" The coin toss may have left us playing the first half headlong into a 20 mile per hour wind, but Mike's response never wavered: *"Just what we wanted!"*

Mike's optimism was contagious, and our captain, Abby Odom, soon took over for him. Following the coin toss, as she returned to the bench, Odie would shout, "Just what we wanted!" without even bothering to tell us what exactly it was that we got. Her teammates would cheer and everyone would get whipped into a frenzy and still no one knew which end we were defending.

It was our way of saying that we weren't going to let the haphazard flight of a coin affect how we were going to approach the game. We won the coin toss or we lost it. Either way, there was nothing we could do about it, and we refused to worry about the things we couldn't control.

Sometimes we would *lose* the coin toss and have to start the game going headlong into a driving wind. Then the other team would hear Abby shout, "Just what we wanted!" and see my players celebrating. They'd wonder if we understood that we had actually lost the coin toss. Those opponents couldn't figure out if we were confused or stupid. We were neither. We were merely responding with our best possible response – an excitement and determination to win the game.

Brandi Chastain rose to superstardom when she scored the game-winning penalty kick to defeat China in the 1999 Women's World Cup final. The iconic photo of Chastain in her sports bra, clenching her jersey, made the cover of practically every major magazine in the country. She became a national treasure. But Chastain and her teammates almost never had the chance to reach the final, and it was Chastain who almost took it away from them.

In the fifth minute of the World Cup semi-final against Germany, Brandi Chastain passed the ball into her own net to give the Germans a 1-0 lead. And as if things could have possibly seemed any worse, Chastain did this in front of 54,642 fans and a television audience of several million, and against one of the best teams in the world. It was every soccer player's worst nightmare. But nothing was going to change what had already happened.

How did Chastain and her teammates respond to the disaster?

Team USA's response to having conceded such an embarrassing goal was to shift into a higher gear. U.S. goalkeeper Briana Scurry told Chastain, "Don't worry about it. Let's get it back." Instead of brooding over their misfortune, the Americans countered with greater determination and urgency and began dominating the Germans.

The U.S. tied the score 11 minutes later and Chastain was nearly off the hook. But just before half-time, Germany again took the lead and everyone knew that if the U.S. were to go on to lose the game by a single goal, all fingers would be pointing at Chastain. At half-time, Brandi Chastain decided she would make an impact.

Four minutes into the second half, Chastain, who had not scored in her previous ninety-nine international appearances, volleyed a blistering drive off the post and into the German net to tie the game at 2-2. The U.S. would go on to win that game by a score of 3-2, eventually putting Chastain in a position to win the World Cup with one swing of her left foot.

Winners know that you cannot change the past. You can only respond to it. And no matter how you feel at that moment of despair, you always get to choose how you will respond. Winners know that regardless of the magnitude of the disaster, they still get to consciously choose their response.

When you are dealing with the uncontrollables, you still have a choice. Winners choose to respond with their best.

PART 4
THE DIRTY WORK

If you want it badly enough, you'll do what you need to do to win. This is where the competitor trumps the player. A competitor is willing to embrace an attitude that a player will not. The competitor understands that the sole purpose of competition is to separate the winner from the loser. That simple premise is the competitor's GPS.

The dirty work is where competitors separate themselves from players. These are the things we expect from boys but rarely ask of girls. And until you prove that you are emotionally capable of playing in the muddy end of the field, you will be forever underestimated and undervalued.

So the only question you really need to ask yourself is this: How much does winning really mean to you?

17

Get into Character

"Nice guys finish last."
                        - Leo Durocher

The opponent was semi-conscious and lying near the sideline. The referee stopped the clock. My players wandered over to our bench while the trainers tended to the injured opponent who had the misfortune of being matched up against Joelle Zucali. Joelle took a quick drink of water then nonchalantly announced, "Well, I don't think we'll have to worry about her anymore."

We had been playing for fifteen seconds.

No foul was called because there was no foul. Joelle saw a chance to line someone up and so she did. It was a brutal, fair tackle, and Joelle had no regrets about it. As a matter of fact, she enjoyed that part of her job. For Joelle, it was just another day at the office.

Joelle was a sweet kid. She was very kindhearted, popular, a fantastic student, and she would be the first one to help out a friend or volunteer for a community service event. But when it was game time, Joelle became someone else. And that's one big reason we won a lot of games. It wasn't that Joelle knew more about winning than anyone else; she was just willing to *do* more to win.

As for you... I like you. You've got a warm heart and you're great with kids and puppies and you always say *please* and *thank you* and sometimes you bake things and they are delicious. Now, please remember that none of that does me a lick of good when it's time to play soccer. When it's time to play, I want... No... I *need* you to dig deep and become your nastiest, most ruthless self, and attack your opponent with venom and rage and disproportionate force. In short, I need you to become someone else. Can you work with me on this?

This is a principle that women have a harder time executing than men. That said, I have coached many female players who have made the conscious choice to get into character when it was time to compete. Like all the principles in this book, it's just a matter of making a decision. The players who managed to consistently get into character always became the core of my teams. They were the players I wished I could keep forever.

Every coach loves a player who has an alter-ego: Off the field, she is a model citizen who gets along well with her teammates and excels in the classroom. On the field, she morphs into a win-or-die competitive monster that will run over anything that stands between her and victory. In women's sports, those Jeckyl and Hyde personalities are few and far between, and that's what makes them so incredibly valuable.

When a coach says it's time to switch on, he means it's time to let that freakish alter ego take over. This is getting into character. It's not difficult to do, but it takes a conscious decision that a lot of players forget to make day after day after day. A team is always on its emotional edge when it faces certain rivals, but that's easy. The player who remembers to get into character for the *boring* opponents and for the daily training sessions is the player my team cannot do without.

In the summer of 2005 I went to a play called Red Light Winter at Chicago's Steppenwolf Theater. The production is set in Amsterdam and has three characters, two American men and a French prostitute. The prostitute and one of the men are very likeable. But the other man is a despicable jackass who continually dehumanizes the woman. By the end of the play, everyone in the audience utterly despised this guy.

My friend worked as the stage manager at the Steppenwolf. After the show he introduced me to Gary Wilmes, the actor who played the character that the audience had grown to hate. Upon our introduction, the very first words out of Wilmes mouth were, "I'm not really like that."

He wasn't kidding. Wilmes was actually a really nice guy, charming and polite, nothing like the villain we had watched on stage. But Wilmes is so good at his craft, so convincing in his role as the heartless villain that he actually has to introduce himself with a disclaimer! When he steps onto stage, Wilmes has a role to play. He's created an alter ego for his character and he lets that alter ego take over. And if he didn't, he wouldn't be nearly as good at his job.

When you step into the arena of competition, you are stepping onto a stage. You have a role to play, and that role is not as the kind, generous, compassionate person that you normally are. Your role is the nasty, competitive monster that will do everything in her power to find a way to win. On that stage you have the freedom to be whatever superhero or super-villian you choose.

You've got to give yourself permission to assume an alter ego when you are in the competitive arena. As a matter of fact, it is your responsibility to step into that new character. It requires neither permission nor forgiveness from anyone other than you. The competitive arena is a different theatre. The rules are different. The consequences are different. Therefore, you too, must also be different. You've got to play your role on that stage. Give yourself permission to be the greedy, nasty conqueror that your job requires.

Chances are, at some point or another, you've played with or against a player like this. They're the ones who coaches describe as fiery. They are the ones jawing at everybody on the field. When there's a controversy on the field, they always seem to be in the middle of it.

In college I had a teammate who was a particularly fiery player. One of our coaches referred to him as a tent player. I asked, "What the heck is a tent player?"

He said, "A tent player is a guy you'd rather have inside of your tent peeing out than outside of your tent peeing in." What he was really saying was that although my teammate wasn't the most talented, we were all better off playing with him than against him.

There are players who, regardless of their talent level, claim responsibility for the pace and intensity of training sessions and matches. They don't just do it once in a while; they do it every day. They view it as their job and they know how valuable that job is to their team. So every day they take five seconds of their lives to say, "My teammates need *me* to be the emotional leader today. I am going to do that job." And you know what it takes to do that job? Simple. A willingness to stir the pot. That's all. It's just a decision that one player makes while another one doesn't.

We've all known those tent players. They are the players you hate but secretly wish you didn't have to play against, as in – wouldn't you be excited to have that player on *your* team? They are the players that opposing fans love to hate.

As someone striving for championships, you need to separate who you are from what you do. For a certain amount of hours each week, your sport is your job. It is what you do. It is not who you are. Excelling at the job of winning often requires you to adopt a different set of values than you would display, for instance, at the family dinner table.

Imagine a Thanksgiving dinner where, as soon as the food was placed on the table, you started grabbing everything in sight as fast as you could and refused to share it with anyone else. Your grandmother wants some turkey and your Uncle Jack wants the mashed potatoes and Aunt Pearl wants the cranberries, but you've gotten to them first and pulled them close and are threatening the others with your utensils, because you don't want anyone to get a bite of that meal except for you. Congratulations! *You are winning Thanksgiving!*

Obviously this type of behavior is unacceptable in your home (If it isn't, move.). But it is exactly this type of ultra-greedy mentality that is critical to your success in the arena of competition.

Winners know their character. A winner's uniform is more than a show-piece – it's a costume. When a winner puts on that costume, the compassionate citizen goes away and the diabolical competitor assumes command. Winners immediately recognize when there is a competition and reflexively they snap into character.

It is equally important to get into character for training sessions. When the coach says, "We're going to play a little one against one," that's exactly what the average player thinks: *I'm going to PLAY some one against one.* The winner's reflex response is *I MUST WIN this game of one against one.* The player who remembers to step into character at training makes her team better because she forces everyone to play at a higher level or suffer the consequences, namely humiliating defeat. Give her the chance and she will beat you 100-0. In a collision sport like soccer, that player forces everyone to think and play faster or risk their legs. That player is invaluable because she makes training sessions fast and intense and emotional when they otherwise wouldn't be. She forces teammates out of their comfort zones the same way an opponent will on game day.

As our team grew into its success, there was no player more important than Joelle. Joelle, more than any player I've ever coached, was superb at getting into character. She loved being the bad guy. She was fearless and mean and she understood that she could influence the game with her physicality. She understood how one big hit could turn momentum in our favor. She took it upon herself to dish out the first big tackle in every game. She didn't wait for physical contact to happen; she went looking for it.

I cannot tell you how many times over the course of Joelle's career, a teammate of hers said to me after a game, "I was a little bit flat today and then Joelle creamed that girl and it got me all fired up." I've never had another player who so motivated her teammates, or another captain who was so respected by them.

I'll go to my grave saying this: Winners will do the things that are necessary to win. They'll do the dirty work that the average competitor won't do, and Joelle bathed in the dirty work.

The need to get into character was a topic we constantly addressed. The people we were for 22 hours a day were not capable of overcoming a more talented team. But the people we could become, the personas that we could create, could beat anyone. Those characters we created had permission to do the dirty work.

Contact sports like soccer, basketball, and hockey give players the opportunity to physically impose themselves on the opponent. There is no net or boundary separating the teams. There is a heavy degree of contact involved, and there are rules governing that contact. There is a line between what is fair and what is foul. It is your responsibility to push against that line at all times.

It is your responsibility to exert as much physical influence as humanly possible on your opponent. Any player who is not constantly testing that line is begging to be defeated. Players who get into character have no problem testing that line every time they compete.

Any player can rise to a new emotional level when an opponent angers her. But the players who can get into character for every single competition, well, those players shine like diamonds. They are invaluable to the atmosphere of a team. Those are the players whose personalities can carry a training session and build a culture of winning. If you can build a team full of those personalities, you will rarely lose anything.

Don't confuse who you are with what you do. Give yourself the freedom to obliterate your opponents because that's your job. Do your team and yourself a favor and get into character.

18

Get Greedy!

"Anyone who thinks $2 million is enough will never make $2 million."

- Anonymous

Winners are different. Their drive to win is unnatural. That's why, by definition, they are not average. When a winner sees a competition, a trigger goes off in her internal circuitry. She immediately blocks out all the distractions. Her field of vision is an ever-narrowing circle, shrinking smaller and smaller, honing in on the target, until her mind sees only the list of solutions to get from Point A to Point B to win that competition. It's like those cartoons where someone sees the opportunity to get rich quick and dollar signs appear in his eyes. Winners have that response, except the dollar signs are replaced with *W*s.

When we were still chasing our first championship, it was a top priority to have the most competitive training sessions in the nation. We weren't talented enough to win on talent, so we needed an equalizer – something to narrow the talent gap. We needed to develop an alter ego for our entire team. That alter ego had to be a greedy, greedy winner. One of the philosophies I hammered into the players was that they never had to apologize for winning – not in games, and not in training. Guiltless greed became a reoccurring theme for our team meetings.

You've got to see your career as a bank account for winning. Each game is an opportunity to deposit a win in your account. At the end of your career, you want the number of wins in that account to be as high as possible. When your career is finished, you want to be able to look at that account and admire how full it is with your deposits. The greedier you get, the bigger your account becomes.

When the players began buying into this, we began winning more games by more goals and putting the games out of reach much sooner. When we got greedy, winning was no longer just an objective; it was an emergency! And that mindset drove our team to extinguish opponents as quickly as possible.

The players also discovered that greedy isn't just about winning on the scoreboard; it's also about winning all of the little battles during the course of competition. It's about hogging all of the joy for your team and sharing none of it with the opponent. It's 90 minutes of gimme, gimme, gimme!

During one pre-game talk I wanted to hammer home the point of hogging the joy. I told the team that winners don't worry about being nice and they don't make apologies for their successes. Winners know that regardless of what their detractors say, if you are a winner, there isn't anyone who wouldn't rather be in your shoes than the other guy's. We had blown some opportunities that year, and if we hadn't, we would not have gone into that match 7-4; we would have gone in 10-1. But there were days when we were not greedy. There were days when we had gotten complacent and lost. We needed to remember that winners are greedy about winning. It's more than a desire; it's an obsession.

In that pre-game speech I asked my players to take the field greedy and to maintain that standard of greed for every one of those ninety minutes. I asked for a conscious effort to hold ourselves to a standard of ruthlessness regardless of the score or the time on the clock. I didn't want to win most of the battles; I wanted us to win all of them. Holding ourselves to a standard that was simply good enough to beat an opponent wasn't good enough. Our standard had to be virtually unattainable. We needed players who refused to let that standard drop.

That is why the highlight of that match came with one second left to play, and it was delivered by our 5'2" central defender, Abby Odom.

We had routed our opponent on the scoreboard. We were winning 7-0 and the Public Address announcer was counting down the final ten seconds. We had the opponent pinned deep in its own end. One of their defenders managed to slide a ball up the middle of the park towards one of their forwards who was still fifteen yards on their side of midfield. The player receiving the ball could do us absolutely no harm whatsoever. There was only one second left in the game; she was seventy yards from our goal, facing the wrong direction, and we had a seven goal lead. But I hadn't asked for winning to be our standard. I had asked for greed.

Instead of letting that team leave the field feeling like they had the ball when the game ended, Odie came flying in, slid around the girl and tackled the ball away before that opponent could get a touch. Time expired as the ball rolled away. It was beautiful!

That was exactly what I meant by holding ourselves to a higher standard! Odie could have very easily sat back and done nothing. Time would have expired and no one would have been the wiser. But in that instant, she refused to let our standard drop. She refused to let that opponent feel any more joy than absolutely necessary. Odie chose to make a battle where there didn't have to be one, and she chose to win it! She had a chance to suck a little more joy out of the opponent's evening and she took it. It was greed in all of its magnificent glory!

As insignificant as that moment may seem, I consider it to be one of the big turning points in our program. It gave me a chance to celebrate a moment where a player decided that being ruthless and winning was better than just winning.

Odie's last second tackle was among the first dominos to tip in our evolution as winners. Our alter egos began to evolve. My players had so much hostility built up from two years of failure that they wanted to do more than beat an opponent; they wanted that opponent to leave the field in tears. That's not an exaggeration. That literally became a goal of our team: Make the opponent cry. When the game ended, my players wanted to see the other team in tears.

When we discovered the competitive monsters we had been harboring within, we all but vaporized the talent gap. To beat us, you not only had to be significantly more talented than us, you also needed to have a very good game. Suddenly we were steam-rolling opponents that were similar in ability. We were beating them on the scoreboard; we were battering them physically; and most important of all, we were breaking their spirits into tiny pieces.

Our new persona had made us the most hated team in the Florida Sun Conference. The players loved it! They knew that although everyone hated us, there wasn't a team in the conference that wouldn't jump at the chance to trade places. We were willing to do the things they were not, and that was their problem, not ours. We would never apologize for winning.

That spring a few of us had volunteered to help with an Easter Egg Hunt. Towards the end we saw some boys and girls who were coming back in tears because they couldn't find any eggs. Parents were racing to console them. It was a heartbreaking sight. Then a little boy came strolling up with a huge smile on his face. He had so many eggs that he had to use the front of his shirt as a basket to hold them all. Right on cue, two of the players turned to each other, nodded their heads and said, "Winner."

Winning is no one's responsibility but yours. You can decide to get greedy or you can accept whatever cards the game deals you. Winners will do the things that make average competitors uncomfortable. They know that during the course of a game there are hundreds of battles to be won, and they want to win as many of them as humanly possible. They don't only want to beat you on the scoreboard; they want to break your spirit.

Winners never apologize for winning. Remember, *greed is good!*

19

Go for the Cut

"The object of war is not to die for your country; it's to make the other guy die for his."
- General George S. Patton

What we do is not about making friends. It's about conquest.

I remember being eight years old, watching a Saturday afternoon boxing match on the television with my dad. One of the boxers had sustained a cut above his eye and blood was streaming down his face. Immediately his opponent began aiming every punch at that cut, and I couldn't understand why. It went against everything I had learned in school, particularly that you help someone who is hurt. In my mind, the other boxer should have started aiming somewhere else. I was very confused.

"Why does he keep hitting that man's cut," I asked my father.

My dad laughed for a second. He realized that I hadn't learned one of the principles of boxing. He explained that when you cut your opponent, you aim for that cut because you have a chance to end the fight. In other words, when you find a weakness, you need to exploit it. This principle is not limited to boxing.

As long as there have been sports there have been coaches struggling to get their players to realize that when you get an opponent vulnerable, you've got to shift into a higher gear and go for the kill. In boxing this principle is easy to observe because it is virtually literal. In other competitions it might not be so obvious.

In 2000 our team had reached the point where we actually had the chance to lead some games. Our inability to finish off our opponents became a major issue for us. As a program starved for wins, it was very frustrating to get the upper hand on a team only to have that team come back to tie the game and eventually win it. We were like the boxer who opens a cut over the opponent's eye and then starts aiming for his shoulders. We didn't recognize those moments when an opponent was vulnerable, so we couldn't exploit them.

My players were still maturing as competitors. They kept stepping out of character at the wrong time, like, while the game was still in progress. Regardless of the frenzy with which they began a game, if we took the lead, they became satisfied. Satisfied people are nice people. We didn't need nice people. I needed the players to understand that there are no points for nice. There are only points for points.

We needed to stop thinking in terms of the scoreboard and to start thinking in terms of the opponent's spirit. Scoring the first goal equates to winning a battle; that's great, but it's very small-picture. The big picture is the crack it puts into the foundation of a team's spirit. That's where the first goal cuts the opponent – in its spirit. If you can knock out a team's spirit, that team loses its will to fight. The sooner you can shatter your opponent's will, the more likely you are to win.

In soccer and many other sports, the spirit-goal relationship is cyclical. You score a goal; you damage the spirit, which should make it easier to score the next goal – which further damages the spirit. Eventually the spirit breaks and that's when the proverbial floodgates open. The key is recognizing when a spirit has become vulnerable and then refusing to give it the chance to heal. When a boxer staggers his opponent, he immediately shifts into a higher gear and begins to fight with much more urgency. He knows that if the injured opponent can hang on until the end of the round, he'll have a chance to heal. So the boxer steps up his tempo and tries to end the fight before the round expires.

I begged the players, particularly our captain Joelle, that the next time we took a lead, we needed to try and end the game right then and there. We needed to smell blood and go in for the kill. If we could break our opponent's spirit, that team wouldn't have the will to stage a comeback.

Our next game was against a team that we had tied once and lost to five times in the first three years of our program's existence. But with each passing defeat, we had inched a little closer to them. By 2000 we had narrowed the talent gap to a manageable margin. Now, on a beautiful October night, Joelle opened the scoring and we had finally taken a lead on our nemesis.

When we got that first goal, Joelle's teammates mobbed her in celebration, but Joelle was having none of it! She shoved them away and immediately began campaigning for more urgency. She was jabbing her finger toward her team-mates and saying, "We're not done! We finish this team right now!" Joelle was tired of heartbreaking losses. She wasn't going to let her teammates forget the lesson about the cut boxer. Joelle wanted to break spirits and she got her team-mates to climb on board. Instead of going from angry to satisfied, we went from angry to enraged. We saw a cut and we began aiming for it with everything we had.

In an amazing display of going for the cut, we scored four more goals in the next eleven minutes to put the game out of reach by half-time. We had scored a first-half knockout. The fight had ended before the first half was over because we recognized a vulnerability and we chose to bombard it. Joelle's goal had won us momentum, and momentum must breed urgency.

There is a saying that a 2-0 lead is the most dangerous lead in soccer. To the average competitor, it may be. For the average competitor, whose effort is a reflection of the scoreboard, a 2-0 lead is often a case of 'next goal wins.' If the trailing team cuts the lead to 2-1, there is often a huge swing in momentum and it isn't uncommon for them to go on and win the game 3-2.

Winners have no issues with a two-goal lead. As a matter of fact, winners love a two-goal lead. Winners recognize a two-goal lead as a bridge to a three-goal lead, and then a four-goal lead, and so on. Winners play with an unbridled urgency to break spirits. That urgency stays with them regardless of what the scoreboard says. When human nature tells us we can ease up, winners instead kick into a higher gear. They don't care if they are winning by two or twelve, that urgency stays with them. If your team is giving away two-goal leads, you have an unacceptable competitive problem because you are measuring your effort against the scoreboard. And that will always spell disaster.

Winners recognize the chance to break spirits, and they don't let those chances pass quietly. When they see a chance to put the game out of reach, they respond with frenetic urgency. The spirit is the head of the opponent. If you chop off the head, the body will follow – and the game is yours.

When the opportunity to slam the door is upon you, slam it! Once you break an opponent's spirit, she is at your mercy. Do not give her the opportunity to heal her spirit before the result is out of reach. Finish her!

Believe me when I tell you, when the opponent bleeds, go for the cut.

20

Be the Bully

"You don't get what you deserve, you get what you take."

- Anonymous

There are places where it's not okay to be a bully. Your school is one of them. It's not acceptable to go around tormenting kids for their lunch money. If you're doing that, *stop right now!*

If you have ever been bullied, you know your first reaction is something along the lines of, *Well that sucked*. Then you have some time to think it over, to stew in your anger, and then you begin to wish the situation could be reversed. Then you wish that you could bully the bully. Hate them all you want, but bullies have one thing every competitor craves – bullies have power. While the rest of us have to go through the necessary channels to meet our needs, bullies just take what they want. In athletic endeavors, that's not such a bad thing.

Bullies operate on a tilted playing field. They are freelancers who attack people who can't stand up for themselves. In the schoolyard, that's disgusting and unacceptable. In the athletic arena, it's absolutely phenomenal!

In sports, the playing field is level. The rules that govern your sport make sure of that. The opponent chooses to step onto that field with you; you aren't backing her into a corner in the hallway. And because she makes that choice to challenge you, you have a right and an obligation to make her pay heavily for that choice. In the athletic arena, you can be a bully taking whatever the heck you want to take, and it's socially acceptable. It's a celebration of guilt-free domination!

The Embry-Riddle Soccer Program was built around a ferocious competitor who I've already mentioned, Joelle Zucali. What separated Joelle from her peers was her grasp of the consequences before the game started. She knew there was the possibility of ending up as the loser. And she used the ninety minutes between the first whistle and the last to do everything in her power to make sure that wouldn't happen.

Joelle had no moral hang-ups about being a bully. One of her goals for every game was to put in the first crunching tackle. She wanted the opponent she was matched up against to be afraid of her and that's what usually happened. Once she had the upper-hand, Joelle was relentless. She was constantly chirping in her opponent's ear, forever reminding her who was in charge.

Joelle was once matched up against an exceptionally fast opponent who blew right by her for the first few minutes of the game. Joelle was pretty fast, but this girl had utterly blinding speed and quickly staked out the upper-hand. But that speedy opponent was also carrying an illness and began rapidly fading after fifteen minutes. It wasn't long until she was hunched over straining hard to catch her breath – like she was on the verge of an asthma attack.

Joelle saw her opening and went for the kill. She immediately announced to the field, "Hey! This girl is dying! She can't run anymore! Get the ball to me!" Yes, Joelle wanted the ball. More importantly, she wanted the opponent to hear her. Joelle wanted her fading opponent to know that the tide had turned and that she had no intentions of letting that girl catch her breath. Joelle went for the cut and became the bully. She repeatedly went bombing forward into the attack at full speed, forcing her coughing opponent to chase her. With each sprint the opponent ran, her wheezing and hacking grew worse. A few minutes later, after Joelle had run by her three straight times, the opposing coach substituted his fastest player out of the game.

Being a bully is an uncomfortable prospect, particularly for girls. You've been socialized from the moment you left the womb to work and play well with others. You've been taught to cooperate, not to conquer.

Winning always involves the conquest of an opponent. And to conquer someone means to make that person unhappy, exactly what you've been brainwashed not to do. The rules of competition are like the black outlines in a coloring book in the hands of a seven-year-old. For the most part the crayon is going to stay inside the lines. But that crayon will still make occasional forays outside of those lines. That's where the dirty work is. Often times the margin of victory can be found along the fringes of those lines.

Winners understand that not everyone is willing to do the dirty work that is required of conquest. Not everyone can switch off the personality that has helped them grow into a socially well-adjusted, likeable person. Not everyone can step into a character whose sole mission is to dominate and conquer another human being. Not every player can make herself genuinely believe that second place is genuinely unacceptable. Winners give themselves permission to conquer. Winners will do the dirty work and happily exploit the opponent who can't or won't make that same emotional sacrifice. Winners don't mind breaking hearts.

Before your contest begins you get to make a choice: Am I going to be the hammer or the nail? Ask anyone who has been beaten up by the bully, it's no fun being the nail. Winners have no problems being a bully. And they do it sooner rather than later.

21

Know Your Enemy

"If you know the enemy and know yourself, you need not fear the result of a hundred battles."

- Sun Tzu

K now your enemy. The Chinese General Sun Tzu said those words in the sixth century B.C. Information has always been power.

Nearly every principle in this book deals with making any game a winnable one. It's about making the unknown a little less unpredictable and exerting influence whenever and wherever possible. It's about manipulating every variable that you possibly can to sway the odds in your favor. In gambler's terms, it's about stacking the deck. And there is no better way to stack the deck than by getting to know your opponent.

Every athlete has tendencies. These tendencies highlight their strengths and avoid their weaknesses. Even high level athletes will go to great lengths to avoid performing those techniques that they are not confident of performing.

It is your coach's job to get you as much useful information about your opponent before the game begins. It is up to you to make good use of that information and to learn more about the opponent and make adjustments as the game goes on. But while you are focusing on an opponent's technical and physical weaknesses, don't ignore that space between her ears, because for many players, that's the soft spot. The 2002 regional championship was a shining example of how to make an opponent unravel.

On the night before the game, we reviewed every one of our opponent's players including their name, jersey number, position, strong foot, weak foot, and weaknesses. There were three players we keyed on, but the most important was a speedy forward named Belinda. Besides being fast and talented, Belinda was a great instigator, very much like Joelle who had graduated from our program.

Belinda was a bully – a great one! She was at her best when she could bait opponents into retaliating against her. As soon as an opponent retaliated, Belinda knew that she was in that player's head and that was where she would do the most damage. It started a psycho-emotional cycle that put Belinda in command and turned the opponent into an emotional pile of goo. If we let her take charge of that game, we were going to lose.

But Belinda had a weakness of her own. Ironically, she too was prone to emotional meltdowns. If an opponent went after her first, Belinda would implode. If an aggressive opponent proactively brought the war to Belinda, she would seem confused, as if to say, *"It isn't supposed to happen like this!"* She would get agitated and lose focus and just wander around the field like she wasn't quite sure of where she was supposed to be.

Once an opponent got into her head, Belinda's posture would change. She would stand on the midfield stripe with her hands on her hips. That was the telltale sign that she had lost her drive to compete. When her hands went to her hips, Belinda became a very average player. If we could get to her before she had a chance to get to us, she would be no good to her team.

Our plan was to agitate Belinda right from the start. Anyone who had the opportunity to make physical contact with her was instructed to do so, regardless of whether or not it was actually necessary. We weren't trying to hurt her or even make her feel pain; we were just trying to annoy the heck out of her. Even if one of my players was just jogging past Belinda, she was instructed to brush into the temperamental star.

So how did our game plan work?

By this point we had no problems getting into character, so instigating Belinda wasn't a stretch. My players took it as a challenge to see how quickly they could get into Belinda's head and were on the lookout for her body posture to change.

We took a couple of upper body fouls on Belinda in the first ten minutes and took a piece of her sock every time she touched the ball. Anywhere she went, someone would bump into her. At different times, Belinda would just be standing around, watching a ball that was sixty-yards away, and out of nowhere someone would breeze by and brush into her. Before she could retaliate, the player was long gone. Whenever one player ran into Belinda, another player laughed, and that was driving her insane!

Thirty minutes into the game, Fish shouted over to our bench area with a big grin on her face. She pointed at Belinda, who was standing at midfield with her hands on her hips, looking very unsettled. The bully had unraveled much faster than we expected and she never recovered. It was like she wasn't even on the field. In the biggest game of the year, the opponent's best player was a non-factor. We won 2-0.

Every opponent has weaknesses, and those weaknesses aren't always just physical or technical weaknesses. You can also find weaknesses in an opponent's level of courage, her temper, and her concentration. Don't ignore them just because she's a girl or you're a girl or whatever. If you want to win, you've got to exploit your opponent's weaknesses every chance you get. You've got to make her play a game she isn't comfortable playing. If you're going to close the talent gap, you've got to make the opponent play an uncomfortable game.

Learn your opponent's weaknesses and attack them without mercy.

22

Don't Get Beat Twice

I'm insanely competitive. I really am. For me it's chemical. When I lose — at pretty much anything — I feel a rage that is impossible to describe. I don't want to cry or mope or go hide in my room; I want to kick down doors and walls and pretty much anything that happens to be in front of me. I'm not proud of this chemical malfunction; I'm only telling you that so I can tell you this:

Whenever my team loses, I go through the handshake line with a big smile on my face. I congratulate the opponents; I look them in the eye and tell them how well they played and I just smile, smile, smile. That's me — Mr. Sunshine. Believe me, it's an act, because on the inside, I'm thoroughly devastated.

I don't turn on the charm because I'm a *good sport*; I turn on the charm because I know the opponents are already rejoicing in their victory and I refuse to add to their satisfaction. It was my Embry-Riddle team that taught me that.

Remember how I said that one of our objectives was to make the opponent cry? Well, if you were one of those crying opponents, your name came up quite prominently in our locker room after the game. My players didn't feel sorry for you; they laughed at you. They knew they had broken your will and they took great delight in dancing upon your grave. You see, winning the game was fantastic, but seeing you in tears made it that much sweeter. They'd beaten you on the field, and then they beat you again when the game was over. It was like getting two wins for the price of one. And knowing how my players relished those moments when your spirit broke into a million little pieces, I refuse to give someone else's team that same satisfaction. So, as much as it hurts, I'm going to paint a big smile on my face and congratulate you on a job well done. I'll reserve my grief until you're far away. When your team plays my team, you may win the game, but there's no way on earth I'm going to give you the satisfaction of beating me twice.

Look, if you want to cry, I'm not going to talk you out of it. But there is a time and a place and you need to remember that. Don't give anyone the chance to beat you twice. Manage your emotions. Take some pride in yourself and refuse to give the opponent permission to dance on your grave. They won the game; you don't owe them anything else. The more it hurts you, the more they're going to enjoy it. Refuse to give them that satisfaction. Cowboy up and put on a brave face and leave the field with your head held high.

PART 5
A TEAM LESS
ORDINARY

Think about all the teams in your league or your county or your state. The teams are more similar than different. The players are all basically the same age; they receive the same amount of coaching; they play the same amount of games. But only one of those teams will ultimately rise to the top. For your team to claim the kingdom, you've got to find a way to separate yourself from the pack. You've got to carve out some type of separation between you and those opponents of similar ability. You carve out that separation by creating a team culture that is unmatched by your opponents. You find a way to make it mean more to you than it does to them. Then you live that culture day after day after day.

23

Redefining Sportsmanship

Our practice field was located next to the student-athlete parking lot. For the other athletes to get into the field-house, they often had to pass by our training sessions. The intensity of these sessions would often cause passersby to stop and check out the commotion. It was a lot like stopping to watch a car wreck.

One night, some of my players were hanging out with a few of the volleyball players. One of the volleyball players commented that she could never be a part of our team. She said she couldn't understand how our players could yell at each other so much and still be friends. My players took that as a compliment. A big one. They wore it like a badge of honor. Translated, what the volleyball player had really said was that to be a part of our group, you needed to be something more than ordinary. Membership in our group came with a higher emotional price tag, and my players took tremendous pride in being part of a team where the players were so demanding of one another. At the time, we were the university's only women's team that was winning championships. The volleyball player had justified everything we'd done to win them. And winning those championships all started with a conscious choice to redefine sportsmanship.

If I asked you your definition of sportsmanship, what would you say? What words would come to mind? You'd probably come back with words like *fair* and *nice*. That's what we've all been told it means to be a good sport. Well, I think we can do better. Actually, if we want to win championships, we need to do better.

When two boys go to training, they'll happily kick the crap out of one another to achieve supremacy. The instant training is over, they turn the page and move onto the next thing in their life and they leave the field with their relationship undamaged. Girls aren't so lucky.

One of the major problems with being a girl is that you're on a team full of other girls, and there's an excellent chance that many of those girls take the sport home with them. These less competitive players get offended when they are demolished by the more competitive players, and that leads to episodes of social upheaval. To sidestep these landmines, the more competitive players dial down their thunder during training sessions. The less competitive personalities don't rise; instead, the more competitive personalities sink in order to maintain a more stable social harmony. When part of your training objective is to not offend your teammates, you have a serious competitive problem. A team that drags this type of social anchor is going nowhere fast. If your team is going to win games and win championships, the most competitive personalities need to rule the roost and everyone needs to gravitate up to their level. It won't happen any other way.

I'm going to tell you a story that literally changed my life, and I hope that it also changes yours.

In my third game as a college soccer player, I matched up against an Englishman who was a few years older and many, many years more clever than I. He was mean and nasty and spent the entire game pointing out how much better he was than me. This guy drove me completely bonkers! By the end of the match I wanted to rip off his head and kick it into a lake!

When the game had ended, as my team walked off the field, our captain noticed that I was losing my mind and came over to investigate. In a blind rage I rambled on about what a jackass that guy was and how he did this to me and how he did that to me and how I wanted to strangle him. When I was done spewing, the captain calmly asked, "Did you shake his hand?"

The question froze me. *No, of course I didn't shake his hand. I wanted the guy dead.*

The captain looked me dead in the eye, poked me in the chest and said, "That guy just gave you a day you will never forget. He brought out emotions in you that made this game worthwhile. You owe him a thank you. You should've shaken his hand *first*."

What an enlightening moment! That little speech totally changed my view on competition. I had been looking at it all wrong! The bad guys were actually the good guys because they forced me to bring my best or suffer the consequences. They gave me the experiences and the battles that I would still talk about twenty years later. The bad guys forced out all of these powerful emotions, and in the end, that is ultimately the joy of playing, competing, and winning – the emotion. Emotion is why you do what you do, and why you keep coming back day after day. If you can accept that, you understand the value of your team's most competitive personalities and you value the opportunity to compete against them in training. Then you want to become that type of player because you know how much it means to your team. And suddenly, *sportsmanship* has a whole new meaning.

In our soccer program, on the first day of each preseason, we agreed to change our definition of sportsmanship to this: *It is your job to do everything in your power (short of intentionally injuring me) to beat me by as much as you can. If you do not genuinely try to annihilate me, you are robbing me of my chance to feel those emotions that make soccer worthwhile and memorable. You are responsible for taking me to my emotional brink. If you do not do that, you are being a poor sport.*

I'd go around the room and ask every single player if she bought into this philosophy. When she said yes, I'd ask her if she gave her teammates permission to kick the snot out of her. She'd say yes, and all of her teammates heard her granting them that permission. That gave everyone a green light to be a very good sport and kick the snot out of her. It was like that for every player in our program.

This philosophy led to a lot of very intense training sessions. We had a lot of thundering tackles and pushing and shoving and shirt-grabbing. We argued over whose ball it was nearly every time it rolled out of bounds. When Lisa Lundgren scored a goal, she would taunt our goalkeeper, Julie Greenlee. She'd laugh really loud and tell Julie to, "Pick it out!" Then Julie would shout something back at Lisa and kick a dent into the goalpost. When Julie saved one of Lisa's shots, she'd snicker and say, "Nope. Not today, Lisa," as if Lisa was totally irrelevant. It went on like that for three years, and for three years they drove each other mental.

Julie and Lisa were insanely competitive, and by the traditional definition, their training rivalry would never be classified as good sportsmanship. But both players were so determined not to be bested that they forced the very best out of one another. That's exactly the point of redefining sportsmanship.

We were never the most talented team, but I guarantee that few teams in the country experienced the intensity of our training sessions. Most teams played very few games that would rival the intensity level of our training sessions. Players regularly left training with ripped shirts or shorts and blood running down their socks. While a lot of coaches were worrying about how to get their teams to train harder, I was nervous about someone getting a broken leg.

Which is why we had to create a rule.

As important as it is to switch on, it is equally important to switch off at the end of the competition. When it's over, it's over. Then it's time to take off your costume and resume life as a model citizen and loving teammate. That's why we created the handshake rule.

At the end of each training session, before anyone was allowed to pick up a piece of equipment, she had to shake the hands of all her teammates. It was our way of saying that it's over. *I understand why you did what you did and I'm not going to hold it against you when I get back to the dormitory tonight. I forgive you and I thank you.* The handshake rule allowed us to keep soccer in its own container, and it was one reason why Julie and Lisa remained close friends.

When the players bought into our new definition of sportsmanship and decided to leave their battles on the field, our results took off like a rocket ship! We were so much more emotionally prepared for our opponents than they ever were for us. I liked to think that while our opponents were practicing at a country club, we were practicing on an artillery range. While their teams were practicing soccer, we were practicing trench warfare. As a matter of fact, our games were often less emotionally taxing than our training sessions. We attacked opponents without mercy because that's how we trained every day. We existed in a steady state of turbulence, so when games got heated, we were right at home. Our opponents, on the other hand, were trying to figure things out on the fly. It was rarely a fair fight.

You'll never maximize your abilities if the intensity of your training environment doesn't mirror or exceed the intensity of your fiercest games. There's an excellent chance your coach spends a healthy part of his day trying to figure out exactly how to make that happen. Share this chapter with your coach and maybe you'll solve the problem.

24

The Magic of Accountability

What do you do when your teammate is dogging it at training? Do you tolerate it? Or do you stand up to let her know that her effort is unacceptable? Because only one of those two options is going to fix the problem.

There were many elements that formed our culture, and it's impossible to single out just one as the most important. However, if there was one magic bullet to our success, it was the willingness of the players to hold one another accountable. I believe that our willingness to demand excellence from one another is what separated us from our competitors. It is what turned our training environment into a tsunami, and it's what led that volleyball player to say that she could never be a part of our team. Let me put it in the simplest possible terms: My players weren't going to tolerate a teammate's crappy effort. If you backed out of a tackle or ducked a header or didn't hunt a rebound, your teammates were going to jump all over you.

It wasn't easy at first. Confronting teammates is not standard operating procedure for females. Most girls will tolerate an inferior effort to avoid risking a relationship issue. It took a lot of begging to convince the players that they shouldn't accept a lackluster effort from their teammates during training sessions. This is how I put it to the team:

It is your responsibility to win as much as you can, by as many as you can, as often as you can. If you don't feel like doing everything in your power to win, fine. But don't expect your opponent to grant you mercy. She is not responsible for your happiness. And don't expect your teammates to coddle you. You are accountable to them and they are also accountable to you. If you're not pulling your weight and your teammate gives you an earful, don't expect me to come to your rescue. Winners will always be recognized and rewarded in our program. If you want that recognition, all you have to do is win.

We weren't going to handle our under-performers with kid gloves. Everyone was being given the right to hold high expectations of her teammates, and to expect the same in return.

We played a lot of games of 6v6 (5v5 plus goalkeepers). If we were playing a game of 6v6 and a player on Team A was dogging it, she was guaranteed to get an earful from her teammates. It was pretty common to hear someone shouting at a teammate to, "Get your head out of your ass!"

We began to understand the accountability of each individual to the success of the team. A player who was giving maximum effort was no longer inclined to accept less-than-maximum effort from her teammates. We adopted the words of UNC Soccer Coach Anson Dorrance as gospel: *If you lose, I lose, and that is unacceptable.* And once the players bought into the concepts of redefining sportsmanship and holding everyone accountable, we suddenly had the most competitive training sessions I had ever seen. Our daily training environment was more intense than almost any game we would ever play. And that really is the magic bullet.

Fish was one of the first to really buy into the idea of accountability. Her position in the starting line-up was so fragile that she needed her team to shine every day during these 6v6 games. It was important for her to show well at all times, and to do that, she needed her teammates to perform well around her. She was dependent on them for her playing-time survival. Because the stakes were so high for her, Fish had no reservations about demanding maximum effort from her teammates. She was incessantly demanding of them to play at an ultra-high level of intensity. There were no unimportant plays. Everything mattered. Fish wasn't going to sacrifice her playing time on game day because a teammate didn't feel like working hard at training. Any player who wound up on Fish's team knew she'd better bring her very best effort.

Like Fish, you need your teammates to reach your goals, but do you have the courage to confront a teammate who is giving something slightly less than her very best? Boys don't accept mediocrity just to be polite and neither should you! You have a right to expect the very best from your teammates and they have the right to expect the same from you. Learn to hold your teammates accountable and welcome it when they do the same for you.

25

You Are Contagious

"Nothing is so contagious as enthusiasm."
                              - Samuel Taylor Coleridge

It was pretty standard that the players would start off training with a light run around the athletic complex. For five years I watched them jog off into the distance and then return ten minutes later, always in two columns. Then one spring afternoon, as the players were reaching the final hundred yards of their jog, I saw something unusual. They all had their arms raised high over their heads, then all at once, everyone's heads and arms would tilt violently to the left, then violently to the right, then violently to the left, and then straight back over their heads; and they were screaming and laughing the whole time. At first I was completely puzzled. Finally I realized what I was seeing... my players were riding an invisible roller coaster! And they were having a great time doing it! By the time they got back to me, they were energized and excited and ready to train. It was sensational!

The next day they were rowing their invisible boats. A day later they were synchronized swimmers. Every day it was something different and to be honest, I looked forward to seeing what they would come up with next. But the real benefit was the energy level that these journeys into fantasyland produced. After a spin on the invisible whatever, the players were always revved up for training.

If there is one principle that ninety-five percent of athletes fail at adhering to, if there is one decision they forget to make, this is it. If you want to be a winner, particularly at a team sport, I suggest you tattoo these three words onto the back of your hand:

I Am Contagious!

I have an energy. You also have an energy. So does every person we encounter. No one exists independently. We all rub off on everyone we come into contact with. And everyone who we come into contact with also rubs off on us.

As a member of a team, every day you are either an anchor or a propeller. You never just exist. You are either someone who is pushing us forward or you are someone who is dragging us down. There is no in between. You need to accept that you do have an effect on those around you. Like it or not, you are contagious. You need to be contagious the right way. A team filled with players that understand the importance of this principle and act accordingly has a tremendous advantage over the competition.

In 2003 we signed a freshman named Katrina Morgan. Such a leader was Katmo, that in the spring of her freshman year, I named her a captain. It was an easy choice. I've coached several hundred players on various teams and not one of them could match Katmo's enthusiasm. She was constantly the loudest, most active voice at training, forever trying to encourage her teammates and lift the team's spirit. She also invented the invisible roller coaster.

On the soccer field and in our locker room and on our bus and wherever we went, Katmo didn't have bad days. She decided every day that she wanted to be a propeller. She understood that she could influence those teammates who had shown up flat, and that's why she convinced everyone to ride her roller coaster. She did that because she knew it would have a positive effect on our training session.

Katmo was loud and silly and demanding. She took absolute responsibility for her attitude. When Katmo was having a bad day away from soccer, she refused to bring that baggage into our team setting. Every single day of her career, Katmo arrived at the field excited and energized. Her work-rate matched her enthusiasm. She was a one-woman crusade for great days. Her enthusiasm propelled us into a lot of fantastic training sessions and victories.

Lisa Lundgren was another player who drove us with her enthusiasm, turning our pregame preparation into a tribal dance party. She would get the whole team dancing and jumping. She would grab teammates by the collar, shake them and tell them how great they were and how they were going to whoop their opponent. By the time I walked in to deliver my pregame talk, Lisa already had everyone worked into an emotional frenzy. It wasn't by accident. Lisa knew how important it was to get her team energized and she chose to be the one who made it happen.

To this day it still amazes me how many players forget to make a decision about their enthusiasm before they step onto the field. They have no long-term vision. They can't see past the ninety minutes that we're going to be on the practice field. They don't see how those ninety minutes are an investment for game day. For some reason they can't step onto the field and say to themselves, "Today I am taking personal responsibility for the mood and the pace of training." Most players don't understand the impact that they have on the greater good, and they don't understand how their mood can synthesize a domino effect.

Winners realize they are contagious and they use it to their advantage. Winners understand that a single player does make a difference — either good or bad — on the spirit of an entire team. Winners don't just see their contagiousness as an opportunity to influence the spirit of the team; they see it as their *responsibility* to influence the spirit of the team. They make it a part of their job description. It starts with a decision they make before they even take the field.

You have an effect on your team whether you like it or not. You don't have a choice about that. But you can and you should choose what that effect will be.

Winners take personal responsibility for being their teams' propellers. Everyone is contagious, including you.

26

I've Got Your Back

A few years ago I got an email from Lisa. I don't remember a thing from the body of that email, but I'll never forget the words she used to close it:

Love you, mean it.

Lisa

Then as other emails and messages went bouncing around – some to me, some to the group – I noticed that they were all being finished that same way. *Love you, mean it* had become the standard closing for the emails, messages and phone calls in our group. I was – and continue to be – so very proud of how those players took care of one another as teammates, and even prouder that their relationships haven't faded since graduation. Lisa, Fish, Joelle, Mugsy, Mac, Julie, Odie and the others had all finished playing their college soccer years earlier, but they were still intimately connected by the bonds they formed within our team. I couldn't think of a more appropriate motto for those players.

To understand *Love you, mean it,* you have to read between the lines. *Love you* means I love you. *Mean it* means I've got your back. For most teams, that's just a catch phrase. In our team, *I've got your back* was a way of life. We said it; we meant it; and most importantly, we backed it up.

Do you want to know what your coach won't tell you? He won't tell you how frustrated he gets when you let one of your teammates get bullied. He won't tell you that being a part of a team means sticking together and standing up for a teammate who is in no position to stand up for herself. There are battles that your coach can't fight for you, but that doesn't mean he wants you to lie down and surrender.

The date was Sept. 11. I remember because that's my birthday. We were playing a Division I team with bigger, stronger athletes, and in the second half, things started getting really physical. The referee had lost control of the contest and the game had deteriorated into a hack-fest. It was just a matter of time until the pot boiled over. Eventually it did. As players were jockeying for position at the top of our 18, waiting for a free kick from the center circle, a scuffle broke out.

It started with some pushing and shoving and finger-pointing. These tiffs aren't all that uncommon in soccer, so no one seemed too concerned. The teams formed two lines facing one another, with a two-yard neutral zone separating them, and it looked as if all the turmoil had passed. Then one of their players shot across the buffer zone and punched one of my players in the head. She was bigger than any player on our roster, and she stood there, practically posing as she admired her work, fist still clenched, deliberating whether or not to throw a second punch.

It all happened so fast. It couldn't have been more than a second or two, just enough time for me to want to vomit. I was angry at the player who threw the punch. I was sad because my players weren't standing up for their teammate. And I was frustrated that I wasn't in a position to physically protect my players. I remember thinking that a guys' team would never let this happen. Then, an instant later, there was a thud and a wail. The girl who punched my player was flat on the ground, crawling back across the neutral zone to hide behind her teammates. Odie, the smallest player on our roster, had jumped in to stand up for her teammate, and that was that.

That was the first and only fight in my head coaching career, so I spent the rest of the game trying to figure out what I was going say to my team after the game. I knew the fight needed to be addressed, but I didn't know where to begin. Finally I settled on this:

I don't condone fighting in soccer. I'm not proud that there was a fight. I wish it hadn't happened. But I am very proud that when things turned ugly, you stood up for your teammates. No one will ever mess with you again.

That was nearly 15 years ago, so I've had plenty of time to think and rethink what I said that night. And if that same incident happened tomorrow, you know what I'd say? I'd say the same darn thing.

You can't just be a teammate when things are going well. *Teammate* means a lot more than that. A team is much more than a collection of people who show up at the same time each day to play a sport. A true team is one unbreakable spirit committed to a common cause with an unflinching willingness to defend its own. Teams are families driven by purpose, and teammates are family-plus.

On that September night, Odie changed our program forever. From that point forward, everyone knew we would never be bullied again, not on the field and not off of it. Whatever trouble we faced, we would face it together. And that made us fearless.

I've got your back became the fabric of our identity, and it wasn't just about fighting. Heck, it was almost never about fighting. It was about a code – a code that demanded that whatever battle you were facing, you weren't going to face it alone. And that's how we lived.

If we did fitness drills and some players were struggling to finish, the players who finished first would go back out to run alongside of those who needed help, sometimes even pushing or dragging them across the finish line. No one *ever* finished alone. It just didn't happen.

It didn't matter what the battle was, those players were going to fight it together. If someone was struggling with a class, teammates would tutor her. If someone needed a ride, a teammate would either give a ride or lend a car. If someone needed money for books, a teammate would loan it to her. If one player went to get a tattoo, a teammate was going to get one also. And pity the boyfriend who mistreated one of those players. He was dead to our team. Or maybe he just wished he was. And in 2004, when one of our players gave birth, all of her teammates organized their class schedules around the mother's to make sure there was always a babysitter available on campus.

Our 2003 team lost in a penalty kick shootout to end its season. It was Mugsy's senior year and there were over a thousand people watching that game, and almost all of them were rooting for our opponent. What I remember most about that night was Mugsy's resilience and her devotion to her teammates. Each time one of our players missed her penalty kick, Mugsy would dash out of the center circle and run to that teammate. Then Mugsy would drape an arm around her devastated teammate and walk her back to the center circle, consoling her with each step. We missed four kicks that night, so Mugsy was making quite a few trips. The referee kept commanding her to stay in the center circle, but Mugsy kept ignoring him as she jogged by to collect her teammates. She was practically daring that referee to eject her because they both knew it wasn't going to change a thing. Nothing was going to keep Mugsy away from her teammates. I admired Mugsy's defiance because sometimes *I've got your back* means putting your teammates ahead of the rules. Her trots past the referee epitomized the spirit of our team — a spirit that transcended wins and losses. As she was watching her own college soccer career evaporating in front of her, Mugsy's first priority was to comfort her teammates. *Love you, mean it.*

I was proud of those players for so many reasons, but nothing made me prouder than the way they took care of one another. So many days and nights I had the privilege of watching the most madly territorial group of players I could ever imagine. They recognized the strength in their numbers and they refused to back down from anyone. They could scream bloody murder at one another each day at training, but they were also fiercely loyal when an outsider tried to challenge them.

I've got your back wasn't just something we said, it was our culture, and it has lived on long after those players have graduated. I really don't care how it started; I only care that it started and it lasted and that I got to watch it grow.

The only question you should be asking yourself right now is this: *Does that sound like a team I'd want to be a part of?* If the answer is yes, then you're not looking for a team, you're looking for a culture. And as I told you earlier, a culture can start with just one. To have great teammates, you have to first be a great teammate. Your teammates need to know that they can depend on you — *no matter what*. And then you have to spread the gospel.

Any team has the potential for incredible power, but it will never reach that potential until every player can count on every other player to be there in times of need. The greater the challenge you face, the more important it is to face it together. Until your team internalizes the philosophy of *I've got your back*, it's going to lose to the team that has.

There is no greater feeling in sports than committing to a common cause with people who genuinely care about one another. There can be tremendous power in your numbers, but those numbers must be willing to come together to make a stand at the most challenging times. Don't let your teammates get bullied. I'm not saying that you should charge into the fray with fists-a-blazin', but at least make it clear that your teammate isn't alone. Stand up for the teammate who can't stand up for herself. When someone tries to take advantage of your teammate, make it clear that you've got her back.

27

Winners Answer

"You can't run away from trouble. There ain't no place that far."

Uncle Remus

No, you really can't run away from trouble, especially when it's your opponent that's producing it. Your opponent won't stop for you. The game won't stop for you. When momentum turns against you and the game is suddenly filled with problems, you only have one real choice: You've got to answer.

Basketball, more than any other sport, is a game of runs. In many sports, momentum is depicted by a shift in territorial dominance. In basketball, momentum is depicted by a surge of points.

How often have you seen a basketball team that trails by fifteen points come back to tie the game or take the lead? It happens constantly. Winners have the ability to stem that tide of negative momentum and retake control of the game. In short, winners answer.

There was no more vivid example of a basketball team that could answer those negative changes in momentum than Duke University in the early 1990s. The scene typically unfolded like this: Duke has a lead. The opponent goes on a run of unanswered points. Duke cuts the run by making a basket of its own.

Duke retreats into its own half of the court to set up its defense and waits for the opponent to arrive. The Blue Devils emotional leader, Bobby Hurley, crouches low and smacks both palms down against the gym floor. His teammates follow his lead and four more sets of palms smack the floor. Duke makes a defensive stop, takes the ball to the other end of the court, makes another basket, and suddenly the momentum has shifted firmly back in Duke's favor. Duke pulls away on the scoreboard and goes on to win the game.

Duke's ability to consistently answer in a sport that requires a team to answer so often is what separated the Blue Devils from the rest of the nation. It is a major reason that Duke basketball is one of the few sports franchises in the world that has created that aura of invincibility.

What was great about Duke's answer was that we can attach something tangible to it – the smack of palms against the floor. That smack became synonymous with Duke defense. It was their signature. It was the Duke players telling themselves, telling the opponent, and telling everyone watching the game that they were ready to retake control. That was their tangible signal that it was time to dig a little deeper. The smack of those palms turned many basketball games in the Blue Devils' favor. When those palms hit the floor, the opponent may as well have just rolled the ball down the floor to the Blue Devils and waited in their own end for the onslaught to commence.

What's more impressive about Duke's consistency as one of the top teams in the nation is that they are a trophy team. Every basketball playing non-Blue Devil in the NCAA would love to spend the rest of his life telling the story about the time his team beat Duke. Duke never gets anyone's second-best game. Yet time after time they find the ability to answer.

No matter how dominant or more talented your team is, there are times when you are going to have to battle through adversity. Let's face it; the other team wants to win too. They aren't there just to watch you collect your trophy. As a matter of fact, the more you win, the more often you have to face an inspired opponent. To remain atop the heap in any endeavor, you need to find a way to answer.

EVERYTHING YOUR COACH NEVER TOLD YOU...

During the 2004 season I was troubled by a chink in our mentality. We were winning games, but we had lost the drive to break our opponents' will. There wasn't enough urgency to go for the kill when we had the chance. I listed a string of recent results up on the dry-erase board and asked the players to tell me what those results had in common:

Opponent	W/L/T	Score
F.I.T.	L	2-3
St. Thomas	T	1-1
Webber	W	3-1
Flagler	W	3-1
Flagler	W	4-1
St. Thomas	L	2-3

The first answer was that there were no shutouts. That was correct, but the more pressing concern was that in each of those games, the opponent had scored the game's final goal. When the opponent scored, we weren't answering. We hadn't made a priority of breaking their spirit.

I don't want any opponent to leave the field feeling even the slightest bit good about themselves and you shouldn't either. But that's what happens for the team that scores the final goal. They get to be the last team to celebrate. Even if they lose, they take home a small consolation prize, and I didn't want us handing out prizes.

Right then we made a decision as a team that we were going to score the last goal of the game, and immediately we saw a difference. If we were up 1-0, because we weren't guaranteed to score a second goal, the players worked harder to prevent the opponent from scoring. If we were up 2-0 or 3-0, it was the same. But if an opponent did score, we were going to answer.

We won our first game after that meeting 1-0.

Our next game was against a conference opponent called the Savannah College of Art and Design. SCAD was a very good team, but we were on fire that night and staked ourselves to a 3-0 lead. With twenty minutes remaining, SCAD got one back and the score was 3-1. Riding that wave of momentum,

SCAD's players were feeling pretty good about themselves, maybe even thinking of a miracle comeback. What they hadn't anticipated was the new sense of urgency that we were about to uncork. The situation had suddenly become unacceptable. We had made a decision to score the last goal of each game and we were going to make darn sure that we lived up to it. We steamrolled SCAD back down the park and two minutes later the score was 4-1. That's how it ended.

A funny thing happened when we made our decision to score the game's final goal; we won seven of our next eight games and tied the other. In six of those games, including the tie, we didn't concede a goal. Two of those shutout wins came in the regional tournament, which we won to advance to the national championship tournament. In our first round match at nationals, we trailed by scores of 1-0 and 2-1 before winning 3-2.

When we decided we wanted more than just the result, that we also wanted to break spirits, we became a much more dangerous team. When we decided that we would answer, suddenly we stopped giving away the last goal of the match. When we decided it was important, the opponents stopped scoring.

We learned that to be a winner, you've got to be able to answer. We harnessed the ability to answer when we decided it was important.

If there is one quality that builds the foundation to a winner's aura, it's this: Winners answer. We've seen them do it. Chances are they've done it to us. Somehow, when everything is going against them, winners can pull a rabbit out of a hat and steal a result. That's why we never count them out.

Sometimes, when you're beating a team that you're not supposed to beat, there's a little voice inside your head expecting to ultimately lose – as if maybe you don't really deserve to win. When you hear that voice, you know you are playing against an opponent who has that winner's aura. If you are going to create that aura as a competitor, you need to consistently demonstrate the power to answer and like everything else, it starts with a decision.

Winners win because winners answer.

PART 6
NAME YOUR PRICE

You get what you pay for. That old axiom means that the more you are willing to pay for something, the better the product you'll purchase. Competition is no different. Glory doesn't come at a bargain price. You won't find it in the clearance aisle. It can't be negotiated. Glory is the reward for those who are willing to pay the highest price in terms of work rate, courage and relentlessness. You will indeed get what you pay for. So, how much are you willing to spend?

28

Cowboy Up

The players were crossing the finish line of our most demanding fitness test. They collapsed to the ground in succession as they crossed the finish line. All of them groaned. Some of them puked. At least one wet herself. They had pushed themselves to their physical breaking points. Again.

A few minutes later they sat on the grass and stripped off their shoes and socks. Rachael Lund showed off her battered legs. Her shins weren't just black and blue, they were solid purple. The blisters on her feet were red and swollen. She looked up at me and asked, "How's that for war-paint, Coach?" Soon the others joined in to compare the disfigured limbs that used to be their legs. It was 2003, and it was a year like none other.

In 2003, our team had 14 players — 12 field players and two goalkeepers. Eleven players played nearly every minute of every game, and four of those games lasted nearly 120 minutes. Think about that for a moment. In a collision sport, on a team full of collision players, it's not just unlikely to survive a season with those numbers; it's absurd! It's the nature of our sport that some players will get injured and miss a game or two here and there, and in a sense, we were no different. In 2003, playing an 18-game schedule, we had one player miss one half of one game. That's it. One player, one half, one game. That may be the most remarkable statistic ever in a season of college soccer. But here's the thing... It wasn't like we didn't get hurt. We did. We got plenty hurt. We just didn't get injured, and there's a difference.

If you're injured, it means that you've done some type of real damage to your body and that it's going to get worse if you keep playing. If you're genuinely injured, you should stop playing and heal. However, being hurt doesn't mean that you are automatically injured. Let me simplify it for you: When it comes to soccer, if you can run, you can play. And the 2003 team just kept playing.

Rachael Lund was the toughest of a tough bunch. She was fearless. She played with such reckless abandon that we nicknamed her 'Rock.' When her finger got dislocated during a game, instead of asking to come off the field, she yanked it back into place and kept on playing. Why? Because she had to. She had to keep playing because she was committed to the cause and committed to her teammates.

It was part of our culture to train and play in pain. It was a tradition that began almost by accident on a fitness day in August of 1999. Lisa Lundgren was waiting her turn to run the next repetition of a fitness drill called Six Minutes of Hell. She wiped her chin and called over to me, "Coach, I threw up."

"So what?"

Lisa shrugged as if to say, "Yeah. So what?" Then she kept on running.

At that moment, Lisa sent a message that would define our program for years: *We don't stop just because it hurts.*

Lisa was the first player in our program to heave during a fitness session, but she was hardly the last. And from that day forward, no one tried to use vomit as an excuse to bail on running. It became an unofficial badge of honor for a player to puke or pee herself during a conditioning drill. Plenty did. But they never ever quit. Quitting just wasn't our thing.

You have to understand that in the arena of competition, the winner isn't always the most athletic or the most talented, but *the one who suffers best.* She is the one committed to paying the higher price in the name of victory. She is the one you have to drag off the field because she has a bone sticking out of her leg. She is the one who thinks, 'I'll deal with my personal discomfort after I win the darn game!' And regardless of her level of talent, that girl is a winner!

The point I'm trying to make is that you won't go anywhere as an athlete if you can't fight through some pain. There's a reason we refer to certain athletes as warriors and soldiers, and it's not because they look good in green; it's because of the amount of suffering they are willing to tolerate in pursuit of the mission. Don't underestimate the value of bravery and toughness when it comes to sports. They are priceless qualities and you get to choose whether or not you have them. The 2003 team had them in abundance. That team suffered better than any team I've ever coached. That's the reason those 14 players won a conference championship.

There are some coaches who will rush to your rescue every time you get a boo boo. But eventually you're going to have a coach who expects more and you're going to have teammates who expect more. And when you get to that team, you'd better be able to show that you aren't a crybaby and that your teammates can depend on you — *even when it hurts.*

Because our 2003 roster was so small, we occasionally auditioned someone from the student body who expressed an interest in joining the team. One of these prospects tried out on a light fitness day. All she had to do was run 7 laps around the field in 12 minutes. She collapsed on the third lap. As the other players were running past me, one of them remarked, "Just dig a hole and bury her." The new girl was dead to them. They knew they would never be able to depend on someone who could quit so easily. As much as they wanted more teammates, they weren't willing to tolerate an open-door policy. They'd choose a small tribe of dependable teammates over lowering our standards.

If you want to be taken seriously as an athlete, every now and then you have to cowboy up and show the world that you can be tough. You have to put aside the drama and show that you can tolerate some pain and get on with your business because that's what it takes to be a serious athlete. If you need to roll around on the ground every time someone whacks your shin, soccer probably isn't right for you.

Suffering best means playing through pain. Until you show that you can get knocked down and stand back up, no one will take you seriously. Demand more from yourself. Be something more than just a player; be a hero.

29

Take Your Cuts

"You can't steal second base and keep your foot on first."

~ Frederick B. Wilcox

Teams that win championships have to deal with the fear of winning, so they do. I wanted to make this book about my players, not about me, but because I can't think of a better way to illustrate this point, I've included this personal story.

When I was in ninth grade I played on the junior varsity baseball team at my school. One day I crossed paths in the hallway with the varsity coach.

"Did you bring your glove today," he asked.

I told him it was in my locker.

"Great," he said. "I want you to jump up to varsity for today's game."

I was shocked and elated and feeling just a little bit happy with myself. In my little world of my little private school, this was a BIG deal. For starters, our varsity team was very good; so good that there were only juniors and seniors on the roster. There weren't even any sophomores on the team, yet here I was being called up as a freshman! It was an honor — and much more than that, I had suddenly gotten *waaaay* cooler.

A lot of my friends came to that game and for the first six innings they watched me sitting on the bench. Our team was losing by five or six runs and had only managed one hit the whole game. Figuring things couldn't get much worse, the coach sent me up to lead off the final inning.

The first pitch I saw was a fastball right down the middle of the plate. I took a big cut and smashed that sucker into the gap in left-center field. In my first at-bat as a varsity baseball player, I had a stand-up double. *Look at me go!* I stood on second base trying not to smile, but on the inside I had already anointed myself king of the world! My social status had just skyrocketed! If the game ended right then and there, that would have been fine and dandy with me.

That hit sparked a rally and after eight more batters, we had cut the lead to a single run. It was my turn to bat again and this time the bases were loaded. The day had already been fabulous. Now, with two outs and the game on the line, I was about to be the hero. *Freshman Hero.* I liked the sound of that. This day just kept getting better!

Because we were down a run, the coach had me taking a strike, meaning that I wasn't allowed to swing the bat until the pitcher had thrown me a called strike. The first three pitches were all out of the strike zone. I was up in the count 3-0 and my remarkable day just kept improving. *He's gonna walk me,* I thought. *He's gonna walk in the tying run.* Finally the pitcher threw a fastball down the middle - the exact same pitch I had hammered the first time around. But as instructed, I watched it sail by and heard the umpire belt out, *"Steeeeee-rike one!"*

It really should have been no big deal. I already had a day to remember. I'd been called up to play with the big boys and I impressed my friends with a big hit. That called strike was the first hint of adversity I had seen all day. And even if I wanted to swing at it, I wasn't allowed. Besides, it was just one strike. I was still way ahead in the count. I should have been overflowing with confidence.

But the moment that umpire shouted, "Strike," everything changed. Suddenly there was a blown fuse in my internal circuitry. In that instant I stopped thinking about all I had to gain and I started panicking about everything I was sure to lose and everyone I was about to lose it in front of. And for the rest of that at-bat, just as the pitcher was about to release the ball, the voice in my head kept repeating one phrase over and over: *Please be ball four.*

Life doesn't work that way.

The next two pitches were called strikes and just like that the game was over. We lost. I struck out looking. When it mattered most, I had watched the last two strikes fly by with the bat on my shoulder. My great day was suddenly not so great. As a matter of fact, it was suddenly pretty awful.

After the game the coach took me aside and offered me a quote from Shakespeare:

"A coward dies many times before his death, but the valiant never taste of death but once."

I understood.

That at-bat changed my life. When the game was on the line, I didn't even make a stand. When it was time to boldly rise to the challenge, I went into hiding. The shame I felt was overwhelming. I never wanted to feel that helpless again. From that day forward I would refuse to wish for charity from the gods. Right then I made up my mind that no matter how high the stakes, no matter how big the event and no matter how strong the opponent, I was going to take my cuts. If I was going down, I was going down swinging!

I have coached so many teams that have had similar moments. They surprised so many people, including themselves, by thoroughly exceeding expectations throughout the season; then they come upon a critical game, one that will put them in position to win a championship, and suddenly everyone starts hoping for soccer's version of *ball four*. Everyone plays timid and tense and tries passing on the responsibility for winning to their teammates and what you are left with is a winnable game that goes down as a loss.

Every up-and-coming team will face that moment when all the good that's been done can be quickly undone with one loss. How you approach those moments will determine whether or not you win trophies.

No one backs into great achievements. It just doesn't happen. When the moment finds you, you've got to want a piece of it. When the moment finds you, you've got to want to be center stage. You've got to want to see that fastball so you can knock it over the wall and be the hero.

Sure, you may lose. And if you do, so what? If you play with courage and aggression in a genuine effort to win, then at least you can walk away with no regrets. *The valiant never taste of death but once.* Besides, if you don't play like that, you're going to lose anyway. At least lose in such a way that you're not left wishing you weren't a coward.

All those games you've won put you in a fantastic position, but other than that, they're disposable. The second those games have ended, they cease to matter. When you start trying to hang onto them, you're doomed to fail. Those results are in the past and there's nothing you can do to protect them. You've got to let them go and devote all your focus on what you still have to gain. It's the only way.

You don't get to be a winner by playing not to lose. You only get to be a winner by attacking every opportunity to impose yourself on the game.

You're a competitor. The moment will find you. One day it certainly will. When it does, don't watch it fly by with the bat on your shoulder. Dig in and take your cuts. You'll be much happier with yourself. And you'll be much more likely to win.

When it's your turn in the spotlight, stand tall and take your cuts!

30

What Would You Do for $1.5 Million?

"It's not hard to be great. It's just much easier to be average."

- Unknown

C oaching has taught me how a player wants to feel when her last game comes to an end. The problem is that I know this before she ever will and I've got to convince her to believe me before it's too late. I want her to understand how much it really does or really will mean to her. For example, I know she wants to win a national championship but that she isn't always consciously willing to pay the physical price that such an endeavor entails. I know that when she is on the verge of puking that she still has something left in the tank, because she's not puking yet.

A few days before we opened preseason camp for 2005, I literally had an awakening. I was reading Lance Armstrong's wonderful book, *It's Not About the Bike*, and the purpose of my life jumped off the page. My purpose in life is to convince college athletes of the following:

1. This is the best you will ever be. You'll never be fitter, more alive, or stronger. You'll never feel better about your physical self.
2. You will never be as emotionally attached to anything (save for your own family), as you will be attached to this program.
3. Your identity will never be so strong. Your celebrity will never be as recognizable as it is in the bubble of college athletics.
4. This is your last great chance to move people's spirits; to bring them to their feet; to take them to a better place when they are counting on you to bring victory to the university. That won't happen when you're working at XYZ Inc.
5. You have this incredible opportunity to do great things with great people. These are the last significant teammates and coaches you will ever have.
6. You'll never wear another uniform that matters so much (except for our military personnel).
7. This opportunity only lasts for four years.
8. When it's over, you don't get it back.
9. Four years is shorter than you think.
10. You'll regret it forever if you waste it. Forever.

Urgency. That one word is why I was put on this earth in this capacity. My purpose in life is to get my players to understand this opportunity, this four-year window, and to attack it with tremendous urgency.

I've been coaching college soccer for 24 years and all of my players have one thing in common: none of them won their final game. They've all lost a game to finish their collegiate careers. That moment when a player's career dies is a window into her competitive soul.

Upon learning they are dying, terminally ill people are said to go through five stages of grief. Athletes, whose careers have just died, leapfrog directly to Stage Three – Bargaining, where they try to negotiate with a higher power for an extension of their playing days.

Our seniors have put in countless hours of hard work. They've pulled muscles and torn ligaments and spent nights packed in ice. They've spent an eternity on buses and vans rolling down the interstates and back roads. They've sprinted until they've puked, wiped their chins, and then sprinted more. There were days of physical agony they thought would kill them. Then suddenly a whistle blows and just like that, their careers have died. All of the grueling work is over. No one will ever again ask them to run until they vomit. Their muscles will never again burn with agony. They will never again have to do severe physical labor. And at that moment, there is not a thing in this world they wouldn't trade away for just one more day of it. That's bargaining.

At that moment, maybe for the first time in their lives, they have clarity — and they finally realize what soccer was truly worth to them. Unfortunately it took the end of their careers to provide that clarity. But given a second chance, they all vow that they would work harder and spend more time improving their abilities because if they had been just a little bit better, they would have gotten to play at least one more game.

The behaviors you engage in daily are your habits. Your habits determine your path. The most successful players have the best habits, particularly in the areas of training, fitness, intensity, and diet. Improvement is merely the result of forming new and better habits. When you make a decision to improve, there are only two questions that you must ask yourself:

– What am I willing to stop doing?
– What am I willing to start doing?

Those two simple questions will determine your new habits, but only if you can be true to your answers. If you can stop doing one thing that holds you back and start doing one thing that empowers you, you've created two new and better habits.

You already know how to improve. Every player does. They all know they could spend more time with the ball or attack fitness sessions with more intensity. But precious few are willing to actually take action to change their daily habits. They prefer to stay anchored inside of their comfort zones.

As a competitor, you've got to decide what it's worth to form those new habits. Is becoming a member of the starting line-up enough to change the way you spend a part of your day? Is being a starter worth waking up twenty minutes earlier to go running? Is it worth passing on a television show so you can get into the weight room? Is it worth running harder when you are so tired that you would much rather stop? What mental and physical walls are you prepared to run through? What are you willing to trade away to make sure that your career will last just one more day?

It all comes back to your willingness to suffer best. Sometimes *suffering best* can be translated quite literally, but suffering isn't limited to those moments of immense physical pain. Think of suffering also as all the little choices a winner makes each day, where she exhibits enough discipline to do what's best for the long haul instead of opting for instant and temporary gratification.

Suffering may mean saying no to a slice of pizza when your diet is a concern. It may mean going for a run when it's raining or snowing or really stinking hot. Suffering may mean getting up a little earlier, staying up a little later or saying no to a great party.

I believe that all of us almost always know the right thing to do, but few of us consistently make the right choices. Very few athletes consistently exhibit the discipline that winners do. Very few athletes are willing to suffer best on a daily basis, and that's what keeps them average and at the mercy of the winners. Winners are winners because they know what it's worth and they are consistently willing to suffer best. And isn't that a big reason why we admire them?

One of the quintessential *What Is It Worth* moments an athlete will experience occurs during conditioning. There's no getting around it; one of the prerequisites for being a top-level athlete in almost any sport is conditioning. In many sports, the fitter team wins. Fitness can take on many forms, such as your physical strength or your ability to jump. In soccer, fitness primarily means running. And there are going to be many, many times during a player's career when she is going to have to do that running alone. The ability to push yourself when no one else is there to monitor or encourage you is a tremendous test of your will. What you do when no one else is watching determines whether you manage your comfort zone or it manages you.

When you run, eventually you reach the boundary of your comfort zone. Just beyond that boundary is where you'll actually improve. But when you draw near to that boundary, there is going to be a voice inside your head trying to convince you to take the path of least resistance. That voice will not stop jabbering until you are finished and the suffering has ended. It will tell you to slow down. It will tell you to stop. It will tell you that you're injured. It will tell you that you've done enough for today. That voice will give you a million reasons to stay inside your comfort zone. That voice will beg you to give something less than all you have. And if you listen to it, you're toast!

That voice is The Demon. And when The Demon starts talking at you, you're in a battle of wills. You can't let The Demon be the only voice your brain hears. You've got to send your brain some conscious arguments to combat that Demon!

When my players run through a brutal fitness session, I'll shout two of my favorite sayings:

"If it doesn't hurt, you're not doing it right!" and *"What's it worth to you!"*

Those are the two best arguments I know to fend off The Demon. When The Demon appears, you know you're doing something right because you're almost out of your comfort zone. When you hear The Demon, you've got to respond by working harder. It is only in those steps beyond your comfort zone that you will make an impact. Until you leave your comfort zone, you aren't getting any better, and you need to accept that as gospel.

You've got some time-traveling to do. You've got to look into your crystal ball and decide how much being a winner genuinely means to you. You've got to decide what investment you are willing to make to prolong your career by one more game. Each day that passes before you make that conscious decision equates to fewer drops in your bucket on weigh-in day.

A former boss of mine referred to it as the One-Point-Five rule. Let's say he asked me to do something that I was clearly capable of doing, like getting in touch with one of our athletic boosters about a fundraiser. Two days later, he asks me if I got a hold of the guy. I reply, "I tried, but he never answered his phone." My boss would respond with the 1.5 Rule. He would ask me, "Dan, if I told you that you would get one-point-five million dollars for getting in touch with him, do you think you could have gotten it done?"

It's hard to argue with that logic. For a million and a half dollars I would have slept in the man's front yard. It just wasn't worth that much to me. But the One-Point-Five rule puts doing your best into perspective. In all seriousness, are you legitimately doing your best? Would you be putting in a little more effort if it meant becoming a millionaire? If it meant that you would become instantly wealthy, would you find a way to get it done?

When I first started coaching, I used to feel bad for players who didn't get much playing time. After each game I would look down the bench and see a dejected player and I'd feel bad. I was holding myself responsible for her satisfaction. I was genuinely sad for her.

My sympathy died when it dawned on me that rarely did I have a player who was willing to train above and beyond what we did as a team. If Player A starts out better than Player B and they travel parallel paths when it comes to their training, Player A will always be better than Player B. It's up to Player B to close the gap. And often times, the only way to make up ground is to put in extra training that's in addition to the team's training sessions.

When I realized that my Player Bs weren't doing anything to help their own causes, my sympathy died. They could complain all they wanted, but if it really meant that much to them, why weren't they doing anything extra to help themselves?

It's human nature to crave excellence through the path of least resistance. Athletics is a wonderful breeding ground for desperation. There is an excess of next-big-thing training tools. This gadget will make you faster, this gizmo will make you stronger, and this thing will give you great abs in 30 seconds a day. Everyone wants to believe there is some secret to success in their athletic endeavor. And they're right. There is a secret. It's just not very well kept.

Do you want to know what the secret to success is? *You have to decide what it's worth to you.* That's all! That's it! Once you figure out what it really means to you, then you can start taking control of it. Once you figure out what you are willing to stop doing and what you are willing to start doing, then you can begin to transcend the masses of average players who are stuck spinning their wheels and going nowhere fast.

When you don't feel like turning off the television to go for a run; when you'd rather nap than get in the weight room; when you'd rather spend time at the mall than time with the ball – all you have to ask is: *What is it worth to me?*

When life asks you for a sacrifice, a really small sacrifice in the big scheme, you need to get a clear picture in your head of your last awful feeling as an athlete and you've got to decide if an hour of your time is worth avoiding that feeling in the future. You've got to decide if sitting in front of the television today is worth sitting on the bench in three months. Then you need to make that same decision all over again, day after day after day.

Because most players don't make that decision, most players don't get my sympathy. If you don't like your playing time today, ask yourself what you were doing yesterday.

Right now, an hour might seem like an eternity that you could never work into your schedule. But when you don't get to be a part of the team or a part of the game, you'd give anything to get that hour back and you swear that you would make something of it. But when it mattered, you never decided what it was worth to you. And now it's too late and no teammate genuinely cares that you aren't playing and the team that's beating you really doesn't care that you're losing. You made your choice. There's a difference between working for something and wishing for it.

I once coached a goalkeeper who I'll call Sharon. As a freshman, Sharon was our back-up goalkeeper. She was a pretty good player, but she never seriously challenged the starting goalkeeper for playing time. One of the things holding Sharon back was her weight. The extra pounds she carried hampered her natural athleticism. She was too slow to be our goalkeeper.

Now let me tell you something; if you have issues with your weight, your coach isn't going to point them out. He may dance around the topic and say that you need to work on your fitness or your speed, but no coach in his right mind is going to invite the fury of a female who has just been told she needs to lose weight. If you need to drop a few pounds, that's a problem that you've got to confront on your own, and that's what makes Sharon's story all the more remarkable.

At the end of her freshman year, Sharon had her *Aha!* moment. She decided that she was no longer content with her destiny of forever being a back-up goalkeeper, so she decided to do something about it. She decided what she was willing to stop doing and what she was willing to start doing.

For starters, Sharon stopped being lazy. She spent her summer vacation running twice a day. She started out running one mile in the morning and a mile at night. By mid-summer she was running seven to ten miles a day. Sharon also made drastic changes to her diet. She avoided junk food and snacks and focused on eating healthy, low-fat meals.

When Sharon reported for preseason the following August, she had dropped twenty pounds and was in the best shape of her life. By the end of the season she was in serious contention for the role of starting goalkeeper, a job that she went on to win during the spring semester of that year.

Sharon had to make tremendous sacrifices to get where she wanted to be. She had to say no to a lot of foods that she enjoyed. She had to make time every day, twice a day, to run. It wasn't enough to just make the time to run, she also had to follow through with the hard part – she actually had to do the running.

Sharon's three-month metamorphosis was astonishing. Her teammates were quick to point out how much she had improved as a goalkeeper, and of course, how good she looked. Most importantly, Sharon began getting the playing time she desperately craved. When the games were being played, Sharon got to be more than a spectator.

Each day Sharon had tough choices to make when no one was watching. It would have been much easier to be a little bit lazy and skip a day of running here and there. It would have been much easier to cheat on her diet. But Sharon always reminded herself of what it was worth, and that kept her on the right track. Her determination paid big dividends. Being a part of the starting line-up was Sharon's $1.5 million, and she reminded herself of that each and every day.

This chapter began with one of my favorite sayings: "It's not hard to be great. It's just much easier to be average."

My job is to get you to find within yourself the margin between average and great. My job is to convince you to find the drops of fuel left in the tank, and as you get older, you begin to realize there are always a few drops left, begging to be used. I've never had a player die at training. There is always a little more to give.

Here's the deal: You've got a limited amount of time, talent, and resources. Prioritizing one thing means saying no to something else. Winners understand that it's up to them to choose their priorities. Winners make a conscious choice to decide what winning means to them, and then they make their decisions according to those priorities.

You've got to decide what it's worth. And the sooner the better.

31

All In

"Someone may beat me, but he'll have to bleed to do it."

- Steve Prefontaine

The afternoon was hotter than donut grease as the game crawled through the agony of sudden-death overtime. We were supposed to lose this game and we easily could have. We were outmatched in talent and even more outmatched in manpower. We had no reserves on the bench; hadn't had a single sub available all day. Eleven players had played every minute in the brutal August heat of a windless afternoon in south, South Georgia. Their legs were rubbery; their faces were red and hot to the touch. The opponent, Thomas University, had gone eight players deep into its bench and had been swarming us for the last ten minutes. We weren't going to win; I'd already accepted that. We didn't have the energy to mount an attack. Fatigue had become too prevalent; our legs had quit. We were under siege and hanging on for dear life like a boxer hoping to make it to the final bell. The Thomas winger smacked a sensational cross from the right sideline and we were numerically exploited in front of our goal. They had two players, each over 5'6", waiting on the other end of that cross. Our only defender in the area was a 5'3" spitfire we called Mugsy. Mugsy positioned herself between those two opponents and the trio drifted underneath the ball as it floated to the front of our goal. If either of their players won that header, it was going to end up in our net.

The three players rose up in an airborne scrum, each one snapping her head at the ball, hoping to make the decisive play. The two opponents probably would have cracked skulls if it wasn't for the pillow between them. That pillow was Mugsy's head. Somehow Mugsy had gone up amongst the trees and won that ball to foil the attack and keep hope alive. It took incredible courage because the act was fraught with physical risk. But Mugsy accepted that risk, did her job, and paid a heavy price for it. She left the field with blood pouring down both sides of her forehead.

Two minutes later, Mugsy was back in the game with half a roll of gauze pad wrapped around her head. We hung on for a 1-1 tie.

The enormity of that play could not be overstated. If Mugsy doesn't show that courage our team goes from 0-1-0 to 0-2-0, and we're going to have to deal with morale issues. Instead, we heroically salvage a tie against one of the nation's Top 25 teams and we leave the field feeling great about ourselves. That was in 2003, the year when we had a roster of only 14 players. As I mentioned, those fourteen players went on to have a phenomenal year, defeating all the odds to win our third straight conference championship. I trace all of that season's successes back to Mugsy's header.

In 1775, before the U.S. had declared its independence, a Virginia politician named Patrick Henry was beseeching his colleagues to support a war against England. Committed to creating a new nation free from the tyranny of King George, Henry stood before the House of Burgess and gave one of the most important speeches in American history:

"Is life so dear, or peace so sweet, as to be purchased at the price of chains and slavery? Forbid it, Almighty God! I know not what course others may take; but as for me, *Give me Liberty, or give me Death!*"

Give me Liberty, or give me Death. It became a rally cry for every American willing to risk his life in the pursuit of independence. Those who joined the movement for freedom committed themselves to a doctrine of win... or die trying. In modern parlance, Patrick Henry's sentiment could be boiled down to two words: *All In.*

I first heard the expression *All In* when Texas Hold 'Em poker was becoming popular on television. When a poker player says, "All in," what he's really saying is, "I'm either going to win this hand or I'm out of the game." "All in," means he is risking his poker mortality. I don't think it's possible to say anything more with just five letters. *All In.* There's no mistaking the urgency it implies. It's an absolute commitment to the cause. It's time to let it ride. Do or die. *All In* is the embodiment of the ultimate principle of winning. If you took every principle in this book and rolled them into two words, *All In* would be those two words.

Whenever I explain the *All In* principle to my team, I tell the story of Mugsy's unbelievable header. That one play sums it up.

Before each game I meet with my team in the locker room. I list our three objectives to the match on the big dry-erase board at the front of the room. The first objective never changes. In eight years it has stayed the same. For over 150 games our primary objective is this: *Be the aggressor.* In soccer (and most other competitive endeavors), the team that brings the fight usually wins.

Hopefully you won't ever have to be in a fistfight, but if that day does come and your mind makes that executive decision to do battle, here's some sage advice: Hit first, hit hard, and hit often. I can guarantee you that your adversary's initial reaction is going to be to retaliate. You have to make her seriously reconsider that option because if she does retaliate, you'll be the one in physical jeopardy. So you can choose to go all in and throw that first punch with all of your weight behind it and try to knock her into next week; or you can roll the dice and hope for the best. If you choose the latter option, I hope you have a very sturdy chin.

When the U.S. launched Operation Iraqi Freedom, the first leg of the assault was aptly named *Shock and Awe.* Shock and Awe was a massive demonstration of U.S. military power designed to, among other things, make the Iraqi forces believe they were in an unwinnable war. The Shock and Awe campaign was spearheaded by the 800 cruise missiles the U.S. dropped on Baghdad in the first 48 hours of the war. That's about one missile every four minutes for two full days. In addition to inflicting damage to military targets and infrastructure,

Shock and Awe inflicted incalculable damage to the Iraqi military's fighting spirit. By the end of the first day there was no mistaking the intention of the U.S. military. We were not dipping our toes in the water. We were All In.

It confounds me how often players leave the result to chance by not attacking the opponent with life-or-death urgency from the opening whistle. Why wouldn't you attack her? She's trying to beat you! *She's trying to make you lose!* What could be worse than that? Why wouldn't you try to eradicate that possibility as quickly as possible? You've got to remember that fighting is not the objective of a fight. The object of a fight is to *end* the fight and to do it as quickly as possible. You don't do that by easing your way into the fray. You end the fight by breaking your opponent's will with the immediate use of whatever excessive force your sport permits.

The only thing you have in common with your opponent when the game starts is that you both know that one will win and the other will lose. You then have three periods, four quarters, nine innings, or ninety minutes to do something about it. The urgency with which you attack your objective often produces the margin of victory.

If you plan to win, you had better decide before the first whistle to go all in because you can bet your last dollar that the opponent has already made that decision. Go all in because if you don't, you're going to wish you had. If you're going to leave bullets in the chamber, you may as well hand them over to the enemy. Now, guess what she's going to do with them.

During the 2005 season our team was going through a rough patch. We had lost four straight and by half-time of the next game, we were headed for our fifth consecutive loss. In the first half of that game we had managed one shot. In the second half of the previous game we had taken no shots. That meant that in our last ninety minutes of soccer, we had taken one lousy shot. I was particularly miffed at our forwards who I felt were playing with a lack of courage and responsibility. At half-time of that fifth game, I lit into them.

"One shot! In the last ninety minutes you two have managed one shot! Do you realize that's only one more shot than a dead person would have taken? Do you know what I expect of you? When you take the field, it should look like your life depends on it! When you get the ball, it should look like your life literally depends on scoring a goal! It should

literally look like you've been delivered an ultimatum: score or die! That's the message that your effort should convey to anyone who is watching; that if you don't score, someone is coming to kill you!"

One of those forwards, Jessica Garcia, suddenly had an awakening of colossal proportions and took over the game. In the second half she was unbelievable, untouchable and unstoppable, as if her body had been possessed by the presence of some higher power. Garcia put on a show every time she got the ball, flying past opponents with speed or screwing them into the ground with deception. In the first half she had been invisible. Now she was occupying an entirely different plane of consciousness than the 21 other people on that field. Garcia tore up the opposing defense for 45 minutes and finally managed to score a goal in the last minute of the match.

Garcia made a decision before the second half of that game and it changed her whole season. She went on to have a phenomenal year. And for the rest of that season it looked like Garcia's life depended on her scoring goals for her team. Once she committed to going all in, she became an unstoppable force.

Michelle Akers totally defied human nature - and medical science - during the 1999 Women's Soccer World Cup, particularly in the championship game against China. Michelle, in addition to enduring a dozen knee surgeries, had spent years battling a debilitating case of Chronic Fatigue Syndrome.

Michelle had changed her entire life to accommodate her condition and lead her team into the championship match. To complicate matters, Akers had dislocated her shoulder during one of the tournament's preliminary matches. Her body was a physical wreck going into the final.

Despite all of her physical impediments, Akers was the United States' best player in the championship match. She literally played herself into complete exhaustion, so much so that she had to be stretchered off the field in the first overtime. With Akers unconscious, doctors had to cut off her jersey, pack her in ice, and inject her intravenously with fluids. Akers had practically died to win that game for her country. Clearly Michelle Akers knows what it means to be *All In*.

All In means exactly what it implies – a total mental, physical, and emotional commitment to achieving the objective, regardless of the personal risk.

In 2001, immediately after our last regular season match, I met my team in the locker room and began mentally preparing them for the regional championship tournament. I gave them the following speech:

"From here on out, in every game we play, people's seasons will end, and people's careers will end. Your first job is to make sure that it is the opponent's season or career that is terminated."

The players had never looked at it like that before, but right then they realized how high the stakes were. On that night they committed to prolonging the season and particularly, the careers of our seniors. The only way to do that was to end the careers of other college soccer players. We agreed that our mission for the following weekend was to end as many careers as possible. When we took the field the following weekend, we had no trouble being the conqueror. We had no guilt about doing the dirty work. We were All In. The will to survive had set us free.

Competition exists for one reason and one reason only: to separate the winner from the loser. If you want to be a winner, you need to have a clear conscience about the emotional pain you're about to cast upon the life of your opponent, and then you need to go about causing that pain with everything you've got. Hold nothing back. When it's time to go, go *All In*.

32

It All Boils Down to This

"Winners have simply formed the habit of doing things losers don't like to do."

- Albert Gray

So what is it that makes a winner different? What is it about a winner that continually cultivates the habits that lead to winning? Earlier I promised that I would reveal the secret that separates winners from the herd. Now, this is me keeping my promise. When you think about what makes a winner different from everyone else, it really boils down to this:

Winners defy human nature.

That's it. *That's all there is to it.*

Katrina Morgan taught me that. In all my years of coaching, I've never seen another player who excelled in so many facets of life. Katmo was excellence in every sense of the word. She excelled at soccer – as a player, a leader, a worker and a teammate. She excelled in the classroom. She excelled in the ROTC. She excelled in the community. She excelled in relationships. And she excelled at these things every darn day. Additionally, Katmo was one of the funniest, friendliest, happiest people I've ever met. There was never a sense of stress about her, which I found particularly peculiar in a person who demanded so much of herself. When I mentioned earlier that Katmo didn't have bad days, I wasn't kidding. Katmo was the same enthusiastic, positive life force each and every day. Katmo set the bar so high for humanity, that as a friendly nod to her universal excellence, I began referring to her as a superhero.

As I was writing this book, I thought a lot about Katmo — and about her uncanny ability to summon the drive to be spectacular at everything she did, every single day. I began thinking about her vivacious spirit and her boundless enthusiasm and how she took personal responsibility for lifting the spirit of our entire team every single time we stepped onto the training field. That type of enthusiasm doesn't happen by accident. I had long since decided that it wasn't just a genetic gift to have that much zest for life. I knew that happiness and excellence didn't just happen upon Katmo; certainly not every day. Let's face it — as fantastic as she may have been, Katmo was still human, and no human is consistently wonderful day after day after day. Katmo may have been genetically blessed to a point, but she still had to make choices. For years I wondered exactly how she did it. I wondered how she combated those days when she woke up feeling, well, like the rest of us. I wondered if each morning she woke up, looked herself in the mirror, exclaimed, "Today is going to be a great day," then set about to make it happen.

I wasn't exactly sure how Katmo made it happen, but I was convinced that she had some daily mechanism to remind herself to be excellent. And I thought to myself, *That must be exhausting. It completely defies human nature.*

And that's when it hit me. *It defies human nature!*

Yes! There it was! Surely Katmo's insistence on being wholly magnificent each and every day was exhausting. And more importantly — yes, it absolutely did defy human nature!

That willingness to combat human nature on a daily basis is what set Katmo apart from every other person I had ever met! Katmo wasn't normal. She was gloriously abnormal! She was gloriously abnormal in her willingness to take control of her life each and every wonderful day! *Who does that???*

Every player that I drew inspiration from in the creation of this book was abnormal in some discernible way. Joelle Zucali's willingness to demand the best from her teammates was not normal. Julie Greenlee's contempt for losing was not normal. Elizabeth Fisher's drive to battle for her starting position every single day for four years was not normal. Katrina Morgan's dedication to being our emotional leader each and every day was not normal. The courage of Rachael Lund and Meghan 'Mugsy' Fairbrother was not normal. Nicole Johnston's commitment to hunting rebounds was not normal. These are some of the biggest winners I've ever had the honor to know, and the one thing they have in common is that in at least one aspect of competition, compared to the legions of average competitors, they were absolutely and completely abnormal.

The principles expressed in this book are not intrinsic to the average person. At certain times under certain circumstances, we will all exhibit one or more of these qualities. But to live them each day, as if nothing else mattered, that's what separates the absolute winners from the mediocre masses.

The average competitor may show these qualities some of the time. Better competitors may even show them most of the time. But the winners like Zucali, Fisher, Greenlee, Johnston, Odom, Lund, Lundgren, Morgan, and Fairbrother — they demonstrated these qualities day after day after day in a way that defied human nature. They lived the principles in this book and because they did, they took a team from inception to championships in four short years.

It is human nature to stay inside our comfort zones. In his book *Personal Power*, Anthony Robbins says that we preset our destinies the way we preset the thermostats in our houses. We feel there is a range where we are comfortable. As soon as we begin to fall below (fail) or jump above (succeed) that range, the thermostat switches on and we do what is necessary to get back to a comfortable room temperature. Whether our comfort zones are programmed genetically or through our life experiences, we rarely stray too far beyond their boundaries.

Winners have an uncanny ability to constantly push themselves beyond their comfort zones physically, mentally, and emotionally. Winners are unaffected by the thermostat inside the house. When there's a competition, the winner leaves the house altogether.

It is human nature to search for an easier way. It is human nature to avoid physical risks, not actively seek them. It is human nature to take mental breaks, to get a little lazy here and there, to relinquish control and hope for the best. It's human nature to deflect blame onto others and to occasionally shirk responsibility. It is human nature to rest before you reach failure. It's human nature to take your foot off the gas every now and then. It's human nature to get complacent.

It's not human nature to decide what it's worth day after day after day. It's not human nature to always control all the controllables. It's not human nature to play through pain. It's not human nature to throw the first punch. It's not human nature to determine one's own attitude every single day. We're all plagued with a certain degree of mental and physical laziness. Winners recognize this and they fight it. They make the decisions that all of us are capable of making but too often forget.

All of the principles in this book share one common thread – they all defy human nature. Whether they realize it or not, winners are constantly reminding themselves to defy human nature. It really isn't that hard to be great, but it truly is much easier to be average. Winners spend their life fighting off average. The capacity to make that conscious choice to do the things necessary to win is a winner's most effective habit. Making that choice day in and day out is what makes them special.

It is in your consistent willingness to defy human nature that you will find the margin of victory.

The sum of all the principles of winning is found in your willingness to defy human nature.

33

The Meaning of Life

"If only. Those must be the two saddest words in the world."

- Mercedes Lackey

I'm going to let you in on a little secret: This book isn't really about winning. One of my jobs as a coach is to help my players see into the future. Rarely does a freshman show up with any idea of the big picture. When she arrives for her very first day of preseason in this whole new world, four years seems like an eternity. The mortality of her soccer career has not yet occurred to her. She's never considered the legacy she will leave behind. It's up to me to unveil the big picture.

Have you ever considered that one day your playing career will end? Let me tell you something: Your career is finite. It may seem like you will go on playing forever, but there's an excellent chance that you will never play a truly meaningful game beyond college. For the vast majority of competitive athletes, their competitive life dies before the age of twenty-two. As a college athlete you have four years to accomplish whatever it is you plan on accomplishing in your athletic life. At the end of those four years you can only judge yourself by how you answer these two questions:

Did you do your *absolute best?*

Do you have any regrets about the effort you gave *each and every day?*

If you can look yourself in the mirror with a clear conscience and honestly answer *yes* to both of those questions, then you can be at peace with your career.

One of the most frustrating moments in sport is when your team has lost to a team it was supposed to lose to, then ten minutes later you find yourself saying, "They weren't *that* good. I'd like to have that game back. We could have beaten them."

Well guess what… that ship has sailed. That's the beauty of sport – the immediacy of its results. That's why you need to attack every opportunity to compete with urgency. That's why, before the game begins, you've got to make up your mind that you are going to leave that field with no regrets. You don't get a second chance, so you'd better make the most of the one chance you get.

This may sound strange in a book about winning, but of all the games my teams have won, the game that most stands out in my mind was a game we lost.

It was during the 2002 season against a school from Kentucky called Lindsey-Wilson College. If you've never heard of Lindsey-Wilson, don't be fooled. Coaches in the college soccer world are all too familiar with the amazing teams that LWC has produced. Since 2001, LWC has consistently had one of the most talented soccer teams in the country at any level.

We knew that Lindsey-Wilson was going to completely outmatch us in talent. LWC started eleven international players, many of whom have played for their countries' national teams. Five of their players would go on to be named to All-American teams. My players were just good, hard working soccer players. Their team had legitimate, world-class superstars.

Before the game we talked about how we wanted to feel after the game. We decided as a team, that regardless of the score, we were not going to let the opponent break our spirit. We were going to work as hard in the ninetieth minute as we worked in the first minute. If we lost, we lost. So be it. But above all else, we were going to leave that match with no regrets. If we went down, we were going down swinging.

Lindsey-Wilson took the lead in the sixth minute and it looked like we were in for a very long night. They had been all over us from the opening whistle before finally finishing a chance. If we were going to be true to our word and leave the field with no regrets, the soccer gods were giving us one heck of a test.

As the game evolved, it began to resemble the movie 'Rocky', with Lindsey-Wilson being the heavily favored, polished fighter, while we were the street brawler capable of absorbing loads of punishment. For a while that's all we were doing – absorbing punishment. But we kept hanging around and Lindsey-Wilson couldn't land the big punch to knock us out. We refused to give up that second goal.

The longer we stuck around, the more confident we grew. We began launching some attacks of our own. We were the physical aggressor, and that was frustrating our opponent. Their players were very technically gifted. They favored a soft, clean, free-flowing game. My players were blue collar types that liked to bang bodies. Frustrated by their inability to put us away on the scoreboard, our opponent began retaliating against us physically. A team whose strength was its technical ability began trying to play the game on our terms, and that leveled the playing field. Ever so slowly the momentum was shifting in our favor.

In the middle of the first half, Laura DiBernardi took a nasty elbow to the nose. Blood gushed down her face. She had to leave the field to get the bleeding stopped. On the bench she was given the option to be taken to the doctor or to finish the game with a broken nose. Dibo returned to the field a few minutes later with a tissue stuffed up her nostril and a spare pack of Kleenex in the strap of her sports bra.

We had reached half-time down only one goal, which was a lot more than most of Lindsey-Wilson's opponents could say. We were beaming with confidence. Instead of hoping to merely keep it close, now we wanted to win. Now we believed we could.

We came out on fire to start the second half. For twenty beautiful minutes we were actually the better team. In the 56th minute we equalized. Denise Brolly made a blinding run at their defense up the left-center of the park, drawing a crowd of defenders towards her, vacating our attacking right side. NJ came storming up the right side, and at the last possible second, Denise threaded a magnificent diagonal ball through the heart of their eighteen where NJ planted a first time shot back across the goal and into the net. It was a smashing goal! We had just tied the score against the number two team in the country! Better still, we were dominating them! It was absolutely magnificent!

I wish this story had a happier ending, but it doesn't, at least not based on the scoreboard. Lindsey-Wilson scored with fourteen minutes remaining to win 2-1.

In the end, Lindsey-Wilson was the better team. But we had closed the talent gap as much as we possibly could have. We had thrown our bodies around with reckless disregard and had given one of the best teams in the country all it could handle. We had played like our lives depended on it. And because we did, we could walk off that field with our heads held high and a clear conscience. We had no regrets about what we brought to that field.

You see, before you can worry about winning, you first have to make peace with losing. In essence, that's really what this book is all about. It's not about winning; it's about everything you are willing to invest to avoid losing. It's about deciding that you are willing to do A, B, C & D to the very best of your ability, and if that's not enough, then so be it. This book is about leaving the field with a genuinely clear conscience. Walking off the field with no regrets is the meaning of life.

When you decide that your objective is to have no regrets, you immediately gain a sense of calm because you begin judging yourself on a whole new standard. When you hold yourself to a higher standard than the scoreboard, and that standard is based on giving everything you can possibly give, you begin to enjoy the game at a new level. A wave of nothing-to-lose freedom washes over you. You're not afraid to take risks. You don't hide. You don't panic when it's your chance to be the hero. It's like you're playing the game with your favorite song playing in your head. And the bonus? If you can hold yourself to that higher standard, the scoreboard almost always follows.

If you look at your most recent season or game or match, ask yourself what regrets you have. Did you not get to play as much as you would have liked? Did you not get to be a part of the starting line-up? Did your team suffer through a lackluster season? Did you cower when you had the chance to be the margin of victory? Did you accept mediocrity from your teammates? In my experience, a player's regrets are the sum total of all of her violations of these principles of winning. If you can give an honest, objective evaluation of your performance as it pertains to those regrets, I bet you find the answers somewhere in these pages.

Almost no one goes through her career without a single regret. We're all human and humans are wonderfully fallible. But you will minimize your regrets if you choose your destination before choosing your route.

One of the greatest gifts afforded us by sport is the opportunity to stand up and fight for something we believe in, something that is important to us, while surrounded by people we love. Before your next game, take a good look around at your teammates. Together you get to do something noble and worthy and courageous and heroic. Together you get to reveal your greatest selves to the world at large. You won't get to do that forever. Attack that opportunity with urgency and passion. Play that game like your life depends on it. Give everything you have from the deepest recesses of your body and mind and then dig deeper and give more. It's in there. Dig it out.

Be aware that the most anyone can be left with after a game, a season, or a career is a clear conscience. Then set a course that will leave you with one. At the end of the day, you need to know that when it came to your opportunity to compete, you didn't leave any bullets in the gun. If that is indeed the case, then consider yourself one of the lucky ones. You've given all that can be asked of you. That makes you a winner.

This may be the most important advice of all: If it matters to you, then make sure at the end you are left with no regrets.

PART 7
FOR THE GIRLS

As a female athlete, you face battles that boys will never know. For boys, competition is like a type of socially acceptable cannibalism. *Just win, baby!* It doesn't matter how you get there; the end always justifies the means. It's what we expect of boys, so it is what they expect of themselves. For girls it's not so simple.

Look, I don't care what you've been taught up to this point. I don't care how many of your advisors have tried to soften you. Just remember this: You have the right to want to win as much as boys do. You have the right to compete as intensely as the most intense boy, and you should never feel obligated to apologize for your pursuit of victory. If someone tries to tell you differently, it's his problem, not yours.

34

The Edge

"History is written by the winners."
- Unknown

Each summer I ran a soccer camp for boys and girls ages five to twelve. At these camps the boys and girls were always mixed together during the drills and games. In the summer of 2006, we had a nine year-old camper named Katie who was like no other nine-year old I have ever seen. She was more talented, athletic, and intelligent than most nine-year-olds. On those qualities alone she seemed destined for a bright future in soccer. But what truly separated Katie from every other kid at camp was her desire for physical contact. I have never seen another nine year-old, boy or girl, who so thoroughly enjoyed physical contact on the soccer field. There were many occasions when, had she kept running at full speed, she could have easily outraced her opponent to the ball and avoided contact altogether. Instead, she would momentarily slow down, just long enough to give her opponent the chance to arrive at the ball at the same time she did. Then Katie would produce a thundering slide-tackle to wipe out the opponent. While the opponent went hurtling through midair,

Katie would pop up and race down the field with the ball. She did this as much against the boys as the girls.

I loved watching Katie play. It wasn't just because of the physical risks she would take. She wasn't just some goon out there kicking people. She practically never fouled an opponent. She displayed excellent conduct. She was also exceptionally talented with the ball and far more gifted than most players her age. Her dribbling was superb and her passes were intelligent and accurate. She was a lot of fun to watch with the ball at her feet. But I confess that I most looked forward to those situations where I could see Katie lining up an opponent. It wasn't just the way she walloped her opponents that caught my eye. It was the pleasure she obviously took in walloping them. It was how she went out of her way to take those physical risks. That's what made her different. That's what made her special.

I haven't coached many college players who were as aggressive as Katie. This nine year-old preferred winning the ball *and* crushing her opponent to merely winning the ball. I can't tell you what a rare quality that is to find in any female athlete, let alone one who hasn't yet turned ten! I knew Katie had a gift; and if that gift wasn't handled properly, it would also become a curse.

Katie was wonderful, happy, popular girl. She always had a big smile on her face. She was fun to be around and was always surrounded by friends. But as she got older, she was going to run into a wall of detractors. A girl with Katie's blend of talent and aggression would become a lightning rod for jealousy and scorn from teammates, especially when she got to high school where she would be surrounded by teammates who weren't as talented and competitive. I believed that Katie would be very popular with most of her teammates. Not all of them were going to resent her. But I knew that a few of them would. You know the type of girls I'm talking about: the ones that are more concerned about the party after the game; the ones that judge people by how they dress and who they date; the social Gestapo that controls the membership of the high school 'in-crowd.'

Those teammates weren't going to enjoy practicing against Katie. Winning wouldn't mean as much to them as it does to her. They wouldn't enjoy all the attention Katie was going to get. Katie's coach would put her on a pedestal because she is everything her teammates aren't and that would cause resentment. Her teammates would be envious of the awards she'll receive and they'd get sick of seeing her name in the newspaper. And because they wouldn't be able to beat Katie on the soccer field, they'd fire back in other ways. Specifically, they'd try to cripple her socially. They'd talk behind her back and say what a freak she was. They'd spread rumors. They'd do whatever they could to pressure Katie to gravitate to their own level of mediocrity because the average gather strength in their numbers. If those detractors went unchecked, and if Katie wasn't put in an environment where her gift was constantly nurtured and encouraged, she would eventually cave. That was the battle ahead of her.

At the end of the camp I took her aside and said, "Katie, you are an excellent soccer player. You are a winner and I hope that one day you'll play on my team. But as you get older, there are going to be some girls that don't like playing with you, even if they are on your own team. They're not going to like you because they aren't going to be as talented and aggressive and competitive as you are. They aren't going to understand why you play the way you do. When you meet those people, you are going to have to make a choice about what means more to you – their approval, or being a great soccer player. Do not let them change you. Do not bring yourself down to their level. They are going to want you to be average, just like they are. Don't do it. Not everyone can be great, Katie, but you can. You can be a great soccer player. Don't let them pressure you out of it."

I asked her if she understood and she said that she did. I could tell that she meant it. Katie addressed the issue with such understanding that I wondered if she wasn't already engaged in some of those battles.

Katie, at the age of nine, already had an edge that separated her from the masses of soccer players running around fields all over this country. That edge is what separates the good from the average, and the great from the good. While her peers were still discovering the role soccer would play in their lives, Katie had already established her identity as a conqueror.

I love the quote at the head of this chapter. It's direct; it's harsh; and most importantly, it's true. It doesn't matter how well you played or how hard you worked or how bad the referee was because in the end, to the victor go the spoils. One of those spoils is telling the world about the victory. The winner's account becomes the account of record. If you are on the wrong end of the score-line, well, too bad. You don't get the trophy and the world doesn't want to hear your story because your story is going to be a pitiful panorama of excuses about why you didn't get it done. History really is written by the winners. That's life. Deal with it.

Whenever we lose, I post our opponent's press release about the game around our locker room. I do this for two reasons: One, because their version of the event is often far different than ours. And two, because their version is the only one that matters. It is incredibly difficult to digest an opponent's triumphant perceptions about a game that we had the opportunity to win but did not. I want my players to understand that if they don't want to be at the mercy of someone else's perception, they absolutely must do one thing: Win. The. Game.

There is a reality to competition that most of us have been socialized against since the day we were born: Winners exist in a state of mind that is virtually unacceptable outside of the arena of competition. Winners are merciless. They are bullies. They want what they want and to get it they'll bury everyone else who is chasing it. And they love doing it.

In 2002 we had a game in South Florida against a pretty strong opponent. At half-time I overheard Fish talking about the girl she was marking. Fish was commenting on how unfit the girl was and how she was gasping for air. Fish said, "I hate our fitness days, but at times like this, I am so glad we do them. That girl can't even breathe anymore." Then Fish laughed and added, "Sucks to be her."

Fish, one of the most compassionate people I've ever met, had no sympathy whatsoever for an opponent who was on the verge of hyperventilating. It wasn't Fish's problem. Fish had earned the right to be dominant on that day by doing all the running she had done leading up to that day. Fish was enjoying her dominance. And why not? Like I said, she earned it.

Achieving your competitive dreams requires more than a willingness to extinguish your opponent's dreams; it requires a wanton pleasure in extinguishing those dreams. Winners have a razor sharp edge. They are not only willing to make the opponent unhappy; they take tremendous joy in that endeavor. They are not only willing to break an opponent's spirit; breaking her spirit is a priority. Winners will do whatever is required of them to make those things happen. When my players decided that their goal for every game was to make the other team cry, I knew we were going to win championships. I knew it because it wasn't just talk. They meant it!

I've expressed some strong views in this book. I've expressed some ideas that society is uncomfortable attaching to girls. I've stated views that many coaches won't use when their players are female, and views that will make the average competitor uncomfortable. But you know what? That's what makes them average. Winners aren't uncomfortable with the vocabulary of conquest. Those players and teams that consistently beat their opponents enjoy the freedoms provided in the arena of competition. They aren't hamstrung by social expectations. They lead a guilt-free existence inside the arena because they remember that the sole purpose of any competition is to separate the winner from the loser. The winners I've coached, those true win-at-all-costs warriors, they don't mind the vocabulary of conquest. To the contrary, they love it. And if I were to lump those players together, I would simply say, "These are the ones who get it."

When you lose, you are at the winner's mercy and that is a horrible place to be, and being a girl doesn't make it any easier. I believe that if every one of my players took the time to remind herself of that before each game, we would almost never lose.

If you want to be a winner, you've got to free yourself. You've got to give yourself permission to conquer and permission to enjoy it. You've got to be willing to accept a degree of unpopularity from people who do not share your drive – and there will be many. Remember, when you compete, your job is not to make friends. Your job is to conquer. And don't you ever apologize for it!

If you can embrace the role of unrepentant conqueror and live it day after day, you just may have the edge. You'll know it when you feel it. It will burn like a fire inside of you, driving you forward through all barriers. It will make you fearless and merciless. It will erase every distraction and make you single-minded of purpose. Embrace that edge! Let it consume you! That edge is what will drive you to stave off defeat like your life literally depended on it, and then you will be the one writing history.

35

A Piece of the Pie

"It is a man's nature to solve a woman's problems."

- Anonymous

The final piece of the evolution of the Embry-Riddle soccer culture began at a team meeting on the first night of preseason in 2002. Despite the success we had achieved on the field, despite the incredible facilities we enjoyed, and despite the amazing family that we had created, a bug of entitlement had crept into our camp. There always seemed to be someone with something to complain about. One complained about the cut of the training shorts that had been provided to the players – for free. Another complained about the free shoes she had been given. Day after day there was one trivial complaint after another until I thought my head would explode.

The final straw came late in the 2001 season when one of the players began crying hysterically upon learning that the restaurant in our 4-star hotel didn't offer a salad bar. Seriously. That actually happened. It was clear that on any given day, any one of my players could lose her perspective on how good things really were for us.

I was so frustrated by our growing list of complaints, particularly the salad bar crisis, that I considered changing careers. I couldn't handle the sense of entitlement that had developed in some of my players. I realized that if my players could invent things to complain about, then I was teaching them soccer and nothing more. At the time I didn't feel the slightest bit guilty about thinking *This would never happen on a men's team.*

And that, ladies, is the battle you will always have to fight.

Whenever a petty incident like the salad bar crisis infects my team, there is without fail another coach from our department popping his head into my office to say, *"I don't know how you can coach women. I couldn't do it."* That is the reality of the male perception of females. The majority of men still believe women are inadaptable, weaker emotional beings with a predilection for inventing drama. They may not advertise their views and they may not consciously even recognize them, but believe me, when push comes to shove, they expect less of you. It is the reality of the world in which we live.

As a female athlete, part of your job each and every day is to change that perception, or at the very least, prevent it from growing. Every time you take advantage of opportunities to show your worst self, you are feeding the notion that females don't deserve to be taken seriously. When you show weakness, when you complain about the things that aren't worth complaining about, you are setting back your entire gender. This isn't limited to the sports world either. You'll face these same battles when you arrive in the workforce.

At the start of that team meeting in August of 2002, I stood at the whiteboard and wrote:

"It is a man's nature to solve a woman's problems."

Then I asked the players how they felt about it. Trust me, they didn't like it any more than you do. No one likes feeling in need of rescue. To believe that some people will forever view you this way can be, and should be, terribly aggravating.

My players, sitting there in our state-of-the-art locker room, decked out in their university-provided training equipment, had never known any other life as college athletes. It had always been *this* good to them. The free equipment had always been there for them. Their soccer field had always been lush

Bermuda grass. It had always had stadium lights and a booming sound system. They had no appreciation for the struggles of female athletes that went before them. They had no idea that not so long ago, even within their lifetime, women's athletics had minimal support, minimal funding and almost zero credibility.

By the time my players had reached college, the U.S. Women's National Soccer Team was a national treasure. Mia Hamm was already a celebrity. Nike had already spent millions of dollars on endorsements on the national team players. My players had only known the national team that was brought to them by the media; the celebrities that played in front of tens of thousands of adoring fans everywhere they went.

What they didn't know was the team's history in the 1980s. They didn't know that the badly under-funded national team had stayed ten to a room in rundown hotels in Asia, where the bathroom was sometimes a hole in the floor. My players didn't know that in those days, when the national team traveled, the players had to eat whatever was put in front of them, whether it was a pig or dog or monkey. They didn't know that the players once had to sew their own names onto their jerseys. They didn't know that in the early days, the players were not paid. Those players lost jobs and boyfriends and struggled mightily to build the media icon that America celebrated in 1999. My group of small-college athletes had no idea that the treatment they received at Embry-Riddle was astronomically better than the treatment our national team players, the best players in the world, had received for ten or fifteen years.

It was because of the early struggles of those players and other athletes like them that today's female athletes get treated on par with their male counterparts. When my players show up for the first day of preseason, they are each given their own locker in a beautiful locker room. That locker is filled with shirts and shorts and socks and shoes. And you know what? The players haven't done a darn thing to earn them. They are gifts. Each and every one of them is a gift for doing nothing more than showing up.

When my players report for their first preseason, they are treated with a degree of respect. Those material gifts are the university's way of saying, "Your team is as important as our men's team. You will be treated equally well."

When you report for your first day as a college athlete, you will probably receive that same type of respect. And like my players, you haven't done a single thing to earn it. Not yet.

In the 1980s, the women's national team wasn't playing to sold out venues. They were basically playing in front of their parents and whoever else happened to stroll by. Now, at Embry-Riddle, it is not uncommon for us to play in front of 1,000 or more fans. Those fans show us respect by attending our matches when there are a million other things they could be doing with their time. They are saying that just because you are female, it doesn't mean I won't enjoy watching you play. That is respect. And when you play, you will also enjoy that respect.

The fact that my university even has a women's soccer team is a show of respect to the female gender. The opportunities available to you today were not available to your mother and grandmother. According to the NCAA in its 1981-82 Sports Sponsorship and Participation Reports, in 1981 there were only 80 NCAA women's college soccer teams. There were only 1,855 NCAA women's soccer players! That's only 37 players per state!

In 1990, there were 318 teams comprised of 6,781 players. Does that sound like a lot of opportunity? It may at first, but remember, that's still only 135 players per state.

Now compare that to 2003 when there were 895 NCAA women's soccer teams that consisted of 20,437 athletes! Obviously the growth in women's soccer has given today's players far more opportunities than their predecessors. That growth, fueled by the 1972 passing of Title IX legislation, is a sign of society's growing respect for women as athletes.

That respect was won for you by throngs of female athletes – pioneers that you have never heard of. Players who sacrificed more than you can imagine have given you the opportunities you enjoy today. Those who went before you have won you that respect. It is your job to make sure that you don't give it back.

For decades female athletes have been winning little pieces of respect one moment at a time. The roads they traveled were infinitely harder to navigate than any hill you will ever climb. They were outcasts. They played when it wasn't socially acceptable for girls to play sports. They played against boys because there were no leagues for girls. Some disguised themselves as boys when leagues wouldn't allow girls. They went to court — *to the Supreme Court* — to guarantee that women are given the same opportunities as men. Now, compared to those pioneers, what have *you* done for your gender? Please tell me you've fought the good fight. Please tell me you've done more than just complain when the world hasn't bent over backwards to make your life easier!

The great challenge for the female athlete will always be getting men to take you seriously. It's not fair; I get it. It's nothing you've brought on yourself. It shouldn't be your burden to bear. But it is. That's just the way our world works. It is a disappointing reality to accept, but the sooner you do, the better off you will be.

When I took my first coaching job in 1991, I had no interest in coaching women. All I wanted was a job and I took the one that was handed to me — women's soccer coach. I admit that back then, I wasn't sold on the female athlete. I shied away from telling people what I did for a living. When asked, I would say, *"I'm a soccer coach;"* never, *"I'm a women's soccer coach."* I loved my players and we had a great time and won a lot of games, but I couldn't get myself to accept them as true competitors, certainly not on the same plane as men. I expected less of them because they were women and for a time that's exactly what I got. And I was coaching a team that was ranked in the nation's Top Ten!

But over time I began to change. There were little moments that showed me that I had been ignorant in my judgment. Those moments convinced me that women deserved my respect as athletes and competitors.

When our goalkeeper was unavailable due to injury, we had to put a reserve forward, Keri Alexander, in goal. Keri had never played a day of goalkeeper in her life, but she was willing to do it to help the team. If Keri got injured, we were literally left with no goalkeeper.

With twenty minutes left in the game and us winning 1-0, Keri came out and collided with an opposing player to make a save. During the collision, the opponent's cleat opened up a severe gash in Keri's leg, just below her knee. If the referee saw Keri bleeding, he would have made her leave the game. Keri did not lie on the ground injured. She forced herself to stand up. Then she pulled her sock up high to hide the blood.

We didn't even know about Keri's wound until after the game when she calmly said, "Dan, I need to go to the hospital." Did she ever! Keri had played the final twenty minutes of that match in severe pain with a gash that required a dozen stitches. One player's physical courage allowed us to win that game. Suddenly I began seeing women in a whole new light. Keri had shown a level of courage that dwarfed most men. It was my first great revelation about the female athlete. That's when I knew it could mean as much to a girl as it does to a guy.

That was just one moment where a player won a piece of my respect. There were many others on and off the field, and those pieces of respect kept piling on top of one another until the pile was so high I couldn't deny that women had won my respect as athletes. I had been converted.

Those pieces of respect are so difficult to win. Men get them just by showing up. For women, it's an entirely different story. Winning those pieces practically requires the female athlete to show undo heroism. Unfortunately, those pieces that are so hard to win are so very easy to give back. What do you think would be a man's reaction to hearing about a girl who cried because she didn't like her team's choice in restaurants? The battle for respect is like digging a hole on the beach. You won't make any progress if you keep letting sand slide back into the hole. Any respect won can quickly become respect lost.

How do you contribute to changing one more man's perspective of your gender? How do you inspire one more man to convert? You start by not hemorrhaging the pieces that your gender has already accumulated. You don't let the sand fall back into the hole. You refuse to give back those pieces of respect that you have already won, or more likely, those pieces that have already been won for you.

How does the female athlete keep herself from giving back those pieces of respect? You do it one day at a time, one moment at a time. If you want the world to take you seriously, then you must begin by taking yourself seriously. When men expect less of you, you must refuse to prove them right. You cannot give anyone any excuse to doubt your commitment or your fortitude.

You need to understand that as a female, you have been swept into the current of antiquated stereotyping. You are always representing more than just yourself. Your actions will be viewed as a representation of the entire female gender. Remember the reaction of my colleagues after the salad bar fiasco? Did you notice the precise wording? My fellow coaches didn't say, "I don't know how you coach *that one player*." They said, "I don't know how you coach *women*." An entire gender was held responsible for the actions of one person. Nineteen players were directly lumped into a negative stereotype because of the actions of a single teammate.

You, the reader, as a female athlete, were also victimized. One player indicted all female athletes in the minds of those men who came to hear the story of the salad bar. Those men already expected less of the female athlete and that's exactly what that player gave them.

Your actions, particularly your bad ones, will be seen as a reflection of the entire female gender. It is not fair but that's just how it is. The bar is set higher for you. Your standard has to be practically unreachable. It's your responsibility to affect change and that can only be done one moment at a time.

If you want the world to believe that it is important to you, then you must demonstrate - *by your actions* - exactly how important it is to you. Hold yourself to a higher standard. Refuse to complain. Refuse to backstab your teammates. Refuse to let your personal life explode into a team drama. Refuse to allow yourself a sense of entitlement that the world should cater to your every wish. Refuse to let anyone cast you as the damsel in distress. Show the world that you are strong and resilient! Adhere to your team's rules. Pass your fitness tests. Train on your own. Do everything in your own power to solve your own problems before you ask for a man's help. And when the situation requires physical courage, announce yourself with blinding authority!

By the end of that preseason meeting my players understood their role, not just in the history of women's soccer, but also in the evolution of women. Respect became their driving force. They had a new standard to uphold and they were determined to meet that challenge. My players termed it as the *pie of respect*, and they were determined not to *give away a piece of the pie*.

It was impossible to quantify the challenge of not giving away pieces of the pie. Keeping that respect is a matter of how you live every moment of your life. It's an attitude as much as anything else. It's not only the things you do, but also the things you don't. Thankfully, a few days after that team meeting, we had a tangible incident that called for celebration.

When Laura DiBernardi walked out of her apartment one morning, she noticed her car had a flat tire. Her reflex reaction was to call one of her male friends to come and change the tire. Then, just before she began dialing, she remembered our meeting and had a change of heart and decided that she could change the tire for herself. It was a small moment, but nearly all of those re-spect moments are small. It's not what DiBo did that day for her gender; it's what she didn't do that really matters. She didn't put the idea in one more guy's mind that women are too helpless to change their own tires. And that guy was never given the opportunity to pass that idea onto others. DiBo held onto one little piece of respect on behalf of her teammates and her gender. And that mo-ment was a catalyst for other moments.

After training, when the players were carrying the equipment back to our locker room, it was pretty common for a male athlete to happen along and politely ask whoever was carrying the ball bag if he could carry it for her. The day after DiBo's flat tire, this happened and the ball-toting player accepted the young man's offer. She shook the ball bag off her shoulder and was about to hand it off to the Good Samaritan. Then several teammates started mocking her, shouting, "She's giving away the pie! She's giving away the pie!" The guilty party changed her mind, thanked the boy for his offer, slung the bag back over her shoulder and marched on her way. After that incident, I never saw another player accept an offer to help with the equipment. And why should they? Why should they have asked a man to help them with a problem they were clearly capable of solving on their own? It was one more piece of respect kept.

Those moments spawned many others and a whole new and better culture took root. When the players began demonstrating that they had committed to a cause bigger than just our team, that's when I knew we had reached maturity. That's when the players were learning more than just soccer. When they un-derstood their place in the timeline of women's athletics, they began to take an even greater pride in their role.

Every player has her hardships. Every team has its hardships. How you handle those hardships, the big ones and the small ones, is the measure of your character. Your response to those hardships will be observed and extrapolated as either an indictment or a celebration of the female gender. They are opportunities to show your very best or very worst self. Something that does not go your way is not automatically qualified as a tragedy. Your inability to make the starting line-up means nothing to the terminally ill patient in the cancer ward. Eating at the wrong restaurant means nothing to the starving child. A weak Wi-Fi signal in the hotel means nothing to the U.S. soldier sleeping on the desert floor. Keep your situation in perspective and do the only thing you really can — respond with your very best response.

It is your responsibility to your gender and all of those girls who come after you to positively affect the perception of a male-dominated society. You affect this change by what you do on and off the field. The U.S. national team has affected millions. Keri Alexander affected me. You will have the opportunity to affect others. And those people you affect, they will in turn affect others. What you do in those moments, the decisions you make, will have an effect that will ripple through generations. You represent more than just yourself. You represent the entire female gender. Don't let those moments pass gently. Don't give men the opportunity to cast you as weak. *Refuse* to fuel that stereotype! Don't give back a piece of the pie! Seize those moments to showcase your strength and your independence and your ability to solve problems. Seize them for the good of women everywhere!

AUTHOR'S NOTE

I'm sure that at different points during your reading of this book, you noticed that the timeline seemed skewed. There's a really good reason for that.

Let's begin by sorting out some dates. I coached at Embry-Riddle from 1998-2006. I wrote the core of this book in the spring of 2005. Our team was in a rut and I was exhausted by the lack of intensity we were bringing to our training sessions. For weeks I felt the players were just going through the motions and that our team was going backwards. That passive mentality was driving me to an early grave, so one Sunday morning I woke up and threw a Hail Mary pass by writing down everything I thought I knew about winning. It was 70 pages long and contained nine principles of winning that I felt we needed to address. It called on examples from our alumni who had demonstrated these principles at critical moments in our program's history. I wanted my players to know how we'd won trophies, because it wasn't done on talent, and it wasn't done by just showing up.

I made photocopies for each one of my players and called a team meeting. At that meeting I enacted what I believe to be the first lockout in the history of women's college soccer. I told my players to take at least a week off. I announced that they were not allowed to return to the locker room or kick a ball until we had reconvened as a team. I wanted them to get away from the game for a while and rediscover their passion for competing. I gave them an indefinite deadline and told them not to rush. I asked them to read the packet I had written and to have someone call me when they were ready to start training like champions again. Two weeks later our captain called me and the lockout was over. To their credit, those players came back reenergized and recommitted and we went on to have a productive spring.

Almost every word of that original text is still found in these pages. The title was added years later.

Although I never intended to turn my rant into a published book, I soon realized that my list of principles was comically incomplete – and nothing gnaws at me more than an unfinished project. Over the course of the next eight years, I expanded, massaged, polished and amended these principles and the examples that illustrate them to the point where the timeline became somewhat nebulous. This was always a work-in-progress that could be amended into perpetuity.

The original text was written in the present tense. I left that unchanged where I could, and where I could not, I converted to the past tense. I apologize for the confusion this may have caused you.

I left Embry-Riddle in the spring of 2007 and have not been a head coach since. This became a bit awkward when, in 2014, the decision was made to publish, as currently I am known as the associate head coach at the University of Georgia. To simplify, when in this text I refer to *my team* or *my players* or *how we do things*, I am referring solely to my days as a head coach, and *not* implicating my current boss, Steve Holeman, as an accomplice.

I'd also like to clear up a potential misconception. You may have gotten the impression that because our training environment was so intense, our team chemistry must have suffered. Nothing could be further from the truth. That's one reason I included the story about the volleyball player who said she could never be a part of our team, and how my players wore that like a badge of honor. We were sitting in a van waiting out a rain delay when that story was first told, and when the other players learned of the volleyball player's remark, they laughed out loud and then literally cheered about it. In a strange sense, it justified everything we were putting ourselves through.

Being a part of our team required something just a little bit more, and my players were proud of that. Because the training environment was so intense, it helped to forge intense bonds between the players. As much as I hate to use this example, it's similar to the bond of soldiers who share a foxhole under heavy fire. No one outside the team could fully understand the experience these players were having, so they depended on each other. The intensity of those training sessions didn't push those players apart; it pulled them closer together. I guess what I'm really saying is that regardless of how intense our training environment was, we had a blast, we laughed our heads off, and our team chemistry was fantastic.

The culture described in these pages didn't happen by accident. Believe me, as this culture evolved, every step was by design. I know there are coaches wondering how exactly it was created. If you are interested in learning the specific tools that were employed to feed the competitive monster, I hope you'll read *In My Tribe* (available in 2015). It details all of the leadership concepts that served as the foundation for this culture as well as the exercises used to bring it to life, both on and off the field. It explains the gambles I took, the ones that paid off, and yes, even the ones that backfired. If you want to know how a group of typical female college athletes morphed into a special breed of warriors, *In My Tribe* will give you all the answers.

A FINAL WORD

Thank you for reading my book. I hope you enjoyed it, learned something and feel like you got more than your money's worth. If you did, I hope you will be kind enough to leave me a five-star review on Amazon. Those reviews are an author's currency and it will only take you about 30 seconds.

If somewhere down the road this book affects you or your team in a positive way, I'd love to hear about it. Just email me your story.

If you are interested in buying the paperback version of this book in bulk — at a discounted rate, please shoot me an email at coach@soccerpoet.com.

Thank you to Laura Barlow for the cover art!

Thank you to everyone who contributed to the editing process, especially Scott Arnold, Paul Denfeld, Beth and Sandy Gertel, Chrissy Kanalis, Rachael Lehner, and Rob Marino.

I hope you'll visit my blog at www.soccerpoet.com and that you'll be my Twitter friend @SoccerPoet. If you have thoughts about this book that you would like to share with me, please email me at coach@soccerpoet.com. I do my best to respond directly to each email.

If you'd like to see photos of the players in this book, please visit the SoccerPoet Facebook page.

And finally, I'd like to say thank you to those Embry-Riddle players who in some way, shape or form, got it. It was a blast being your coach. I hope that when my daughter competes, she reminds me of you. Love you, mean it.

OTHER BOOKS BY DAN BLANK

Soccer iQ – Named a Top 5 Book of the Year by the *NSCAA Soccer Journal!* The only book written specifically for soccer players. It details the most common mistakes that players make and provides the better solutions. A few pages from now you can read a sample chapter from this title.

Soccer iQ Volume II – Since Soccer iQ debuted, many coaches have provided suggestions for an awesome second volume, and this is it. Available soon.

Happy Feet – How to be a Gold Star Soccer Parent (Everything the Coach, the Ref and Your Kid Want You to Know) – The book every soccer parent needs to read.

Rookie – Surviving Your Freshman Year of College Soccer – If you're planning to play college soccer, do yourself a favor and read this. I'm trying to help you.

In My Tribe – Developing a Culture of Kickass in Female Athletes   The follow-up to Everything You're Coach Never Told You Because You're a Girl, this book details the specific tools employed to feed our competitive beast. Available 2015.

Possession – Teaching Your Team to Keep the Darn Ball – A step by step explanation of coaching points and on-field exercises for possession soccer. Available Soon.

PRAISE FOR THE AMAZON BEST-SELLER, SOCCER IQ

I *have read just about every book remotely pertaining to the game. After I read your book (twice), I immediately asked my club president for special permission to buy a copy for all my coaches (39 in all). That is how highly I think of what you wrote. You were spot on with every single topic. I think one of the most important things an experienced coach can do is to pass on his knowledge, not protect it. You have done this, and I will do so in turn by providing a copy of your book to my coaches.*

Seamus Donnelly – Director
Penn Legacy Soccer Club

The book is brilliant! I've re-read it three times because I missed a few points the first time. Our unforced errors have dramatically decreased. I'm checking our team budget to see if we have funds available to purchase books for each of the players.

Todd M. Clark – Women's Varsity Soccer Coach
Severna Park High School

Dan what is the fastest way to get 30 copies of your book? I loved the book and I need my players to read it asap.

Joe Hunter – Head Men's Coach
San Francisco St. University

Soccer iQ is the answer sheet for a soccer exam. It's amazing how often these topics present themselves during the course of a game and a season.

Jon Lipsitz – Head Coach
University of Kentucky

I came across your book and cannot thank you enough for writing it.
>Rob Mariani — President
>Cornwall Soccer, Eastern NY

Finally someone wrote this book! If every soccer player read Soccer iQ, every coach would be a lot happier.
>Mark Francis — Head Coach
>University of Kansas

A really great read. Each concept is broken down in a very short and understandable way for players and coaches. I coach girls and it's nice to have a book written from that perspective.
>Don Hutchinson (Amazon review)

Chapter 18

The Shallow End

There are times when you are going to have the ball at your feet and room to run in front of you. And you are going to attack that space with gusto! You'll be in the spotlight. The crowd will stand and cheer and shout your name as you fly down the field with the promise of great things to come. Adrenaline will be surging through your veins! Then you're going to come to a wall of defenders that you can't possibly penetrate – not on the dribble, and not with a pass. You've reached a dead end. Going forward is no longer an option. What are you going to do?

At these moments the average player will get caught up in the excitement and keep ploughing forward and hoping for the best. And as sure as the sun rises and sets, she will lose the ball.

Look, you've got to be realistic about what's happening around you. In the heat of the moment when everything is exciting and chaotic, you still have to keep your composure and use common sense. When the light at the end of that tunnel starts shrinking and shrinking, you've got to have the composure and the common sense to put on the brakes and turn around.

It's okay. Trust me. We understand. And we appreciate the fact that you are helping our team keep the ball as opposed to going on your own little glorified suicide mission. *We get it.*

In these moments it would behoove you to remember a lesson you learned at the swimming pool many years ago. Do you remember the first time you were in an in-ground pool, when you were just a kid and still couldn't swim? You slinked into the shallow end because it was safe there. But you wanted to test your boundaries so you would take one step after another toward the deep end. You'd let the water level come right up under your nose. Then you soon reached a spot where the water was over your head and you realized you were in danger. Then what did you do? You kicked and splashed your way back to the shallow end as fast as you possibly could. And that was a *really* good choice!

The same thing goes for soccer. You've got to realize when the water has gotten too deep and when it has, simply step on the ball and swim back toward the shallow end. Help your team keep the ball. You can't win without it.

Note for Coaches: There is not a doubt in my mind that you have players that suffer from this malady. Every team does. Here's my advice: Get it on video and show your team. Then use the swimming pool metaphor because it's memorable and easy to understand. I've literally had players shouting, "SHALLOW END!" to a teammate who was about to dribble herself into trouble. When players are reciting your metaphors, you know they stuck.

Now, contradictory to everything you've just read in this chapter, a few times in your life you may coach that very special player who can in fact occasionally dribble her way through that human wall. Don't talk her out of it. Just sit back and enjoy the show while she wins games for you.

ABOUT THE AUTHOR

Dan Blank is the author of the Amazon best-seller, *Soccer iQ*, and has been coaching college soccer for over twenty years. He is the first coach in Southeastern Conference history to lead the conference's best defense in consecutive years at different universities (Ole Miss 2009, Georgia 2010). He has an 'A' License from the USSF and an Advanced National Diploma from the NSCAA. You can buy his books and read his blog at www.soccerpoet.com.